Small Businesses Adopting New Accounting Technology

Peggy J. Baker

Abstract

Small business owners often face challenges when implementing accounting information systems, resulting in inefficiencies and reduced competitiveness. The study was grounded in the technology acceptance model (TAM), which guided examination of how small business owners implemented, evaluated, and sustained accounting software use while addressing implementation challenges and leveraging internal and external support. Data were collected through semi-structured interview questions from six small business owners who used accounting software such as QuickBooks, and thematic analysis identified five themes: (a) change management and organizational culture, (b) importance of external support and strategic partnerships, (c) measuring effectiveness through operational and client metrics, (d) challenges and overcoming barriers, and (e) business sustainability and lessons learned. Findings indicated that successful implementation of a company's accounting information system (AIS) was depended on early staff involvement, structured training, and vendor collaboration. Business leaders who integrated technology with people-centered management achieved greater efficiency and client satisfaction. A key recommendation is to develop clear and actionable performance metrics to guide accounting software implementation. The project extends the TAM by emphasizing vendor support and organizational learning as drivers of perceived usefulness and perceived ease of use. Potential implications for positive social change include empowering small business owners to leverage technology for greater economic

resilience, job creation, and community growth.

Table of Contents

Section 1: Foundation of the Project

Small businesses have encountered many challenges in the post-COVID economy and social climate (Akpan et al., 2022). One of the financial hardships that most small business owners faced during and after COVID-19 was liquidity challenges, which made it hard for small businesses to meet their short-term obligations such as payroll and other financial obligations. Small businesses also experienced losses of revenue, sales, profit, which led to employees getting laid off and business closures (Kalogiannidis, 2020). The use of online accounting applications such as cloud computing improved the delivery of services and communications during crisis management such as COVID-19 and played a role in ensuring the profitability, viability and continuity of many small businesses since 2020 (Al-Okaily et al., 2023).

Background of the Problem

Small businesses have been the foundation of domestic and global economies, supported local economies by creating jobs, and provided much-needed products and services to the various communities they served. Small businesses affected the growth of the economy and significantly overall economic success (Akpan et al., 2022). The COVID-19 pandemic caused a major shutdown of economies worldwide, which disproportionately affected small businesses in the United States and the way they functioned (Grover & Sabherwal; 2020, Sastararuji et al., 2022). In 2021, the Small Business Administration (SBA) reported that over 32 million small businesses existed in the United States and that many small business owners were negatively impacted by the

COVID-19 pandemic (SBA, 2021).

Since the COVID-19 generated crisis, the need to implement new accounting technology in small businesses has accelerated (Varzaru, 2022). In order to maintain efficiency and reduce the operating costs incurred because of the constraints imposed by the pandemic, many small businesses were forced to embrace new digital and accounting technologies (Grover & Sabherwal, 2020; Sastararuji et al., 2022). Many small business owners adopted and started using mobile and other collaborative technologies to keep their businesses operational during COVID-19 (Akpan et al., 2022; Papadopoulos et al., 2020).

Business Problem Focus and Project Purpose

Business Problem Focus

The specific business problem is that some small business owners lack strategies to implement new accounting software to remain competitive and avoid business failure. Therefore, the purpose of this qualitative pragmatic inquiry project was to explore the strategies some small business owners used to implement new accounting software to remain profitable in an increasingly competitive business environment after COVID-19. The project was focused on small businesses located in a southern state in the United States, and the targeted population was all members of the small business community in a local city in that southern state.

For this qualitative pragmatic inquiry project, the sample was comprised of six small business owners or managers, and the participants had implemented some type of new accounting software or technology, such as QuickBooks, SAGE, WAVE, or upgraded their existing accounting software or technology in their small businesses since 2020. The participants were chosen from the targeted population using purposive and convenience sampling. Convenience sampling provides the researcher with the ease of access to select participants for the project from the target population (Golzar et al., 2022), while purposive sampling occurs when participants are selected based on specific characteristics (Thomas, 2022).

To gain access to the participants, I used various methods such as networking through various community organizations or online business directories from the local Chamber of Commerce. The participants needed to be aligned directly with the project, as purposive sampling was used to ensure they meet the two inclusion criteria. The two inclusion criteria were being a small business in Tennessee, and the business owners must have implemented or upgraded their existing accounting software or technology in their small businesses since 2020. Aligning participants with the project ensured that the participants would further address the research question using the extant literature, my conceptual framework, and the problem statement. The interview questions in turn were aligned with the research question to elicit the information needed from participants to answer the research question.

Theoretical or Conceptual Framework

This project was grounded in the technology acceptance model (TAM), which provided the conceptual framework guiding the research. The TAM was introduced by Fred Davies in 1985. Using this theory, Davis (1985) investigated the factors that affected users' acceptance of technology in the workplace. The TAM is an adaptation of the theory of reasoned action (TRA), which is used to understand the casual link between user acceptance and actual workplace use of technology.

Two main building blocks of the TAM are perceived ease of use (PEOU) and perceived usefulness (PU; Davis & Venkatesh, 1996). The PU and PEOU of the new or upgraded accounting software should enable small business owners to significantly reduce the time spent on mundane tasks, boosting inventory management and enhanced comprehensive reporting. Small business owners have realized how their businesses could have benefited from the implementation of the software, because small business owners frequently have difficulties adopting technological innovations.

Research Question

What strategies do small business owners use to effectively implement new accounting software to remain competitive and avoid business failure?

Assumptions and Limitations

Assumptions

In qualitative research, assumptions refer to the underlying beliefs and perspectives of the researcher that will influence how they conduct the project (Adler, 2022). The first assumption in this research was that the participants would be knowledgeable about the accounting technology and how such technology had been used to make the business profitable (Clair et al., 2022). The second assumption was that I would have an effect on the project based on which sampling procedures and techniques were selected. The third assumption in this research was that the research participants would be trustworthy, provide honest answers to all the interview questions, and would give accurate and honest descriptions of their experiences (Bryman, 2021). Adler (2022) noted that with regard to semistructured interviews, one assumption is that the interview questions would produce enough data to answer the general research and interview questions.

Limitations

Items that limit the scope of the project or are factors that are beyond the researcher's span of control are limitations (De Oliveira, 2023). Limitations do not necessarily affect the validity of the project and are sometimes outside the control of the researcher. Limitations can include researchers' biases toward the outcomes of the project (Kohler et al., 2022). To reduce such researcher bias, the researcher can report their biases (Coates, 2021).

The first limitation was that this project did not include all business types; only small businesses were used. Sample size was another limitation of this project; the sample size was comprised of only six small business owners, which is not indicative of all small business owners in the area. The second limitation was that only one specific data source was used, which in this case were semistructured interviews. Participant interviews were an integral part of this qualitative pragmatic inquiry project, and these interviews could have been affected by the participants' biases and inability to give accurate information. Some participants could have had reservations on what information they wanted to disclose to an outside party about their businesses. Some participants could have been uncomfortable discussing their business success or disclosing proprietary information that could have given an indication of how well or how poorly their businesses was doing. All these limitations were outside my, the researcher's, control (Campbell et al., 2022).

Transition

In Section 1, I introduced the main facets of this doctoral project, which included (a) the background of the project, (b) the business problem and project focus, (c) assumptions and limitations, (d) the research question, (e) the conceptual framework, (f) the research method and design of the project, and (g) conceptual framework in which the project was grounded was discussed.

In Section 2, I discuss the comprehensive and exhaustive literature review, in which I explore the evolution of the TAM and outline three complimentary and three contrasting theories to TAM. In the literature review, I address the research questions and business problem in the light of the TAM framework. Such information includes implementation strategies for accounting technology, challenges and barriers in implementing accounting technology, the impact of new accounting software on the profitability of small businesses, the impact of COVID-19 on new accounting technology, and strategies for mitigating risks and avoiding small business failure.

In Section 3, I describe the data collection process entailing data collection instruments, techniques, and data analysis process, detailing how I collected, analyzed the data, validated and ensured the data collection instruments were reliable using member checking. I also describe the research method and design, the target population, sample size, sampling methods, address the research ethics using the *Belmont Report,* outline the informed consent process, and how the participants' names and data were protected and kept confidential.

In Section 4, I present the findings and how they addressed the research question as well as their application to professional practice. I also discuss implications for social change and recommendations for practice and future research. Section 4 concludes with my reflections and the analysis of the research data collected in Section 1.

Section 2: The Review

A Review of the Professional and Academic Literature

The purpose of this pragmatic qualitative inquiry project was to explore the strategies employed by small business owners to implement new accounting technologies and to examine how these strategies influenced their businesses' competitive advantage. The literature review synthesizes existing research relevant to the project's central question, themes, and conceptual framework. The literature review provides a comprehensive understanding of the topic in addition to theoretical grounding and context (Kraus et al., 2023). Furthermore, the literature review establishes the need for continued investigation (Paul & Criado, 2020).

The TAM served as the foundational framework for this research and functioned as the lens through which the project's themes and topics were discussed and analyzed. The literature review begins with an introduction to the TAM, including the history and evolution of the model, followed by an explanation of how the TAM aligned with other supporting and contrasting theories and how its main constructs related to the research question. The business problem was addressed by examining the adoption and implementation strategies for accounting software, evaluating the available accounting systems, and concluding with how implementing new accounting technology helped small businesses mitigate risks and increase profitability. Finally, the literature review synthesizes the existing research, provides an overview of how the TAM has been applied in previous studies, identifies gaps in the literature, and highlights potential areas of the TAM for future research.

Organization of the Literature Review

The literature used in this project was obtained from online academic libraries, journal articles, business publications, government reports, scholarly peer-reviewed articles, industry reports, books related to the topic, and dissertations. A substantial portion of the information in the literature review came from academic, peer-reviewed journals. The peer-reviewed status of all journals was verified using Ulrich's Periodical Directory and by reviewing the home page of each respective journal. Access to these scholarly resources was provided through Walden University's online library, which granted entry to several databases, including Emerald Management, EBSCO, ProQuest Central, SAGE Research Methods Online, SAGE Premier, ScienceDirect, ABI/INFORM Complete, and Accounting & Tax.

Table 1 summarizes the number and types of peer-reviewed journal articles and other scholarly sources utilized to fulfill the doctoral project requirements (Walden, 2024). Among the 204 references, 91% were published within the previous 5 years, and 88% comprised peer-reviewed journal articles, consistent with Walden University's standards for doctoral research (Walden, 2025). The literature search employed keywords such as *accounting software, small business, business success, accounting, profitability, competitive advantage,* and *Technology Acceptance Model,* as well as various combinations and derivatives of these terms.

Table 1

Literature Review Sources

	>5 years	2020	2021	2022	2023	2024	Total

Literature type							
Peer-reviewed articles	27	44	41	38	23	7	173
Dissertations	2	1					3
Books	5	3		1	2	1	12
Non-peerreviewed articles	2	5	3	2	1	2	15

History and Development of TAM

Origins of TAM

The TAM served as my conceptual framework, as it illustrates how individuals adopt and use technological innovations. It has been recognized as one of the most frequently applied models in research aimed at understanding user acceptance of emerging and advanced technologies (Vitro & Lopez, 2020). The TAM is effective in explaining user behavior and acceptance regarding the adoption of new accounting technologies (Dziak, 2020; Lee et al., 2003).

The TAM was introduced by Davis in 1986 as the subject of his book while pursuing his doctoral studies at Sloane Business School at Massachusetts Institute of Technology in

1985 (Chuttur, 2009). The TAM is an adaptation of the TRA (Ajzen, 2012), the aim of which is to understand how individuals are persuaded to participate in an activity by projecting the relation between attitudes and behaviors (Davis & Venkatesh, 1995; Lee et al., 2003). The proponents of the TRA argue that an individual's behavior is driven by that individual's intention.

Davis's (1985) book aimed to deepen the understanding of the factors that contributed to the successful implementation of computer-based systems within organizations. The adoption of new technologies in organizations has historically depended on understanding the factors that influence user acceptance and successful system implementation. In his foundational work, Davis (1985) sought to explain why some computer-based systems were adopted while others failed, emphasizing the importance of perceived usefulness and ease of use. During the 1970s, many organizations struggled as newly introduced technologies were rejected by employees, leading researchers to focus heavily on predicting technology acceptance (Chuttur,

2009). These early challenges demonstrated that technology failures were often due not to system design alone, but to human factors such as resistance to change, lack of training, and organizational readiness. Similarly, in the post-COVID-19 era, small businesses faced comparable challenges when implementing new accounting technologies; without proper adoption, these systems threatened profitability and long-term sustainability. This historical and contemporary alignment highlights that understanding user acceptance remains critical and connects directly to examining technology adoption in modern small businesses.

Davis noted three variables in the 1980s as management information system (MIS) success criteria: actual system usage, user attitudes, and performance impact
(Davis, 1985). Figure 1 illustrates Davis's TAM.

Figure 1

Davis's Conceptual Model for TAM

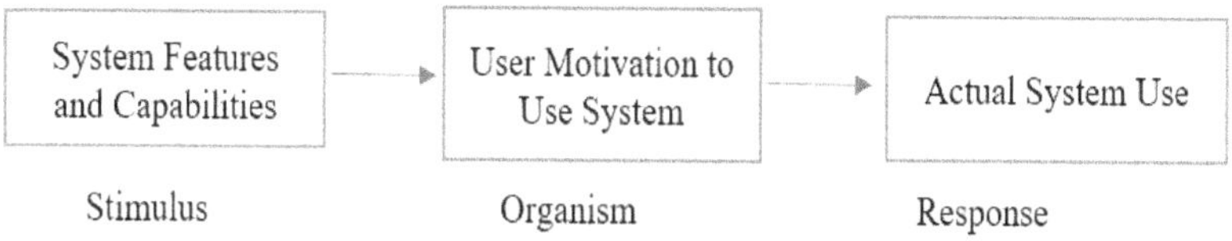

Note. From “A Technology Acceptance Model for Empirically Testing New End-User Information Systems: Theory and Results,” by F. D. Davis, 1985, p. 10.

Davis designed the TAM to explain the motivational process that connects system characteristics to user behavior and actual system use. According to Davis (1985, 1989), the TAM proposed that system features and capabilities function as external variables that influence users’ beliefs, which then shape their intention to use a system. He emphasized that managers and system developers have significant control over these technological features, and therefore play a direct role in shaping user perceptions and acceptance. If users perceive a system as beneficial and easy to use, these characteristics can motivate them to adopt it; if not, they are likely to reject or avoid the system (Davis, 1985). This perspective positions technology adoption not merely as a technical issue but as a psychologically driven process influenced by organizational decisions and system design. It highlights that system success depends on how effectively the system's characteristics speak to user motivation linking external design choices to internal attitudes and, ultimately, to system use or non-use. By framing acceptance as a motivational process influenced by system design and managerial decisions, Davis laid the foundation for using the TAM to evaluate technology implementation across diverse organizational contexts, including modern small businesses adopting accounting technologies post-COVID-19.

Evolution Phases of the TAM

Model Introduction Period 1985-1995. During the TAM introduction period, while user acceptance garnered extensive attention from researchers, the model went through its introductory phase where TAM was replicated with other technologies, longitudinal situations, and research settings to verify whether the model was a parsimonious model (Lee, et al., 2003). **The** TAM was also compared with its predecessor, TRA, to ascertain which model was superior (Lee, et al., 2003). Researchers including Davis found that when compared with its predecessor, TAM better explained the acceptance intention of users than TRA. Also, a comparison of both models showed that TAM offered a slight empirical advantage because it was a much easier, simpler, and more powerful model to use to explain employees' technology acceptance (Chooprayoon, et al., 2007; Lee, 2003).

Model Validation Period 1992-1996. Later the TAM went through a model validation period in which researchers focused on confirming whether the model reliably measured user acceptance across different technological contexts. In this period, researchers conducted studies to validate the TAM's original instruments, showing that the model accurately measured user-acceptance behavior under various technologies, situations, and tasks (Lee, 2003). Some researchers replicated and extended Davis's 1989 TAM project to examine the validity and reliability of measurements for PU and PEOU across different settings and information systems (Adams et al., 1992; Lee et al., 2003). Other researchers found that instead of a two-factor structure with PU and PEOU, a three-factor model including effectiveness as a new TAM variable was more salient (Lee et al., 2003). These findings suggest that the TAM maintained strong measurement integrity and adaptability, even when applied across different system types and user environments, which reinforced its value as a flexible and empirically supported framework. This validation phase strengthened the TAM's theoretical foundation and ensured its continued refinement and use in later technology-adoption research in the model extension period.

Model Extension Period 1994-2000. During this period, new variables were incorporated into TAM research to further explain the relationships between the core constructs PU and PEOU and various external factors (Lee et al., 2003). A distinctive feature of TAM scholarship during this timeframe was the expansion of the model to include external variables related to individual, organizational, and task characteristics. For example, Agarwal and Prasad (1999) extended the TAM by examining five types of individual difference variables as antecedents to PU and PEOU. Their findings indicated that participation in training predicted PU, while prior experience predicted PEOU, thereby supporting the value of integrating external variables into the TAM (Agarwal & Prasad, 1999). These extensions demonstrated that technology acceptance was not solely driven by system design but was also influenced by human, organizational, and contextual factors. By incorporating variables such as individual experience, training, and task characteristics, researchers acknowledged that perceptions of usefulness and ease of use are shaped by a user's environment rather than existing in isolation. This shift advanced the TAM from a purely cognitive model to a more comprehensive sociotechnical framework. Importantly, the success of predicting relationships such as training with perceived usefulness and prior experience with perceived ease of use validated that external variables could significantly strengthen the explanatory power of the TAM. This progression also laid the foundation for future models, such as TAM2 and UTAUT, which further emphasizes social influence, facilitating conditions, and organizational support in the model elaboration period.

Model Elaboration Period 2000-2003. Under TAM II, subjective norms influenced PU and had a direct effect on intentions for mandatory and voluntary usage, which means that as users became more experienced working with a system, they would rely less on social information to form PU, but such users would continue to judge the system's usefulness based on the potential status benefits they would get resulting from the use of the system (Tang & Chen, 2011). Other variables were also defined such as social influence, while cognitive instruments were introduced, such as job relevance, image, quality, result demonstrability, computer efficacy, perception of external control, computer anxiety, computer playfulness, perceived enjoyment, and objective usability (Venkatesh & Davis, 2000). These additions demonstrated that technology adoption was not solely based on functional perceptions, but was significantly influenced by social context, professional identity, emotional responses, and personal capability. By acknowledging that subjective norms diminished over time while status-related motivations persisted, TAM II captured the evolving nature of user acceptance. The inclusion of cognitive and affective variables highlighted that users evaluated technology based on its relevance to their job roles, their confidence in using it, and the psychological comfort or enjoyment it provided This shifted TAM from a purely cognitive model to a more holistic socio-technical framework. As a result, TAM II significantly increased the explanatory power of the original model and paved the way for more unified frameworks such as the Unified Theory of Acceptance and Use of Technology (UTAUT), which further integrated social, organizational, and facilitating conditions.

TAM 3. TAM 3 was developed by Venkatesh and Bala as an expanded version of the original TAM and TAM II, integrating years of empirical findings to create a more comprehensive model of how individuals accepted and used technology. Venkatesh and Bala later proposed a new theoretical framework for TAM which later encompassed the cumulative knowledge accumulated over the years from prior research of the model (Bhattacherjee & Premkumar, 2004). Some studies were conducted to address exiting problems with TAM. The new TAM included four different types of determinants of PU and PEOU, namely, individual differences, system characteristics, social influence, and facilitating conditions (Tang & Chen, 2011). Venkatesh and Bala then put together TAM II with the determinants of PU and PEOU and came up with TAM 3 (Bhattacherjee & Premkumar, 2004). By combining the determinants of PU and PEOU from TAM II with broader psychological, organizational, and environmental variables, TAM 3 acknowledged that technology acceptance is a multi-dimensional process shaped by more than user perception alone. This model recognized that individual traits such as selfefficacy and anxiety, system features, social pressures, and organizational support systems all work together to influence whether a user ultimately accepts a technological system. TAM 3 also addressed criticisms of earlier models by expanding beyond cognitive beliefs to include emotional, environmental, and enabling factors, making it more applicable to real-world organizational settings. As a result, TAM 3 provided a more

holistic and empirically grounded explanation of user behavior, especially in
complex environments where technology adoption depends on both personal motivation and external support. The anchors of TAM 3 included computer self-efficacy, computer anxiety, computer playfulness, perceptions of the facilitating conditions with adjustments such as perceived enjoyment and objective usability. So, TAM 3 is the latest and current model for technology acceptance (Chooprayoon, et al., 2007, Tang & Chen, 2011). TAM 3 addressed the gap extant in the literature on how small business owners or managers make informed decisions about new technologies that can lead to greater acceptance and effective utilization of such new technologies (Tang & Chen, 2011).

Core Components of TAM

Davis's original TAM centered around two core beliefs that determine whether users accept or reject a technology: perceived usefulness (PU) and perceived ease of use (PEOU). At the onset of TAM, Davis proposed two major variables, PU, and

PEOU (Davis, 1986; Lee et al., 2003). PU means, “the degree to which a person believes that using a particular system would enhance his or her job performance” (Davis, 1989, p. 320). While PEOU “refers to the degree to which a person believes that using a particular system would be free of effort” (Davis, 1989, p. 320). These two constructs established that technology adoption is not random but based on users’ rational evaluations of how a system improves performance and how easy it is to use. PU focuses on performance outcomes, while PEOU emphasizes effort and usability, showing that both productivity and simplicity influence user behavior. By framing technology acceptance around these perceptions, Davis shifted the focus from technical features alone to the user’s cognitive and motivational processes.

Davis (1985) also implied that a third factor seemingly affects user’s motivation, which was, the user’s attitude towards using the system. Davis (1989) theorized that a user’s attitude towards a new system would determine if that user accepted or rejected the system (Davis, 1989). The user’s attitude was also influenced by PEOU and PU (Davis, 1985; Davis, 1989). During the evolution of TAM, several variables have been used as a part of the many studies completed to evaluate user acceptance of new technologies. In addition to PEOU and PU, some of the many variables that have been tested using TAM included, effectiveness, relationship between participants in training, prior experiences, role about technology, tenure in the workplace, level of education, managerial support, computer usage, culture, gender, task, user type and social influence (Lee, et al., 2003). The four main variables of TAM have been discussed below, PU, PEOU, behavioral intention, and attitudes. While PU and PEOU were central to predicting user acceptance, Davis (1985) also suggested that a third factor, users' attitudes toward using the system, played a critical role in shaping their motivation to adopt technology.

Perceived Usefulness (PU)

PU represented the first of two primary determinants observed among employees adopting new technology. PU was defined as the extent to which users believed that the utilization of a specific technology enhanced their job performance, efficiency, and goal attainment. It further captured users' perceptions of the accessibility and functionality of the technological system. (Tahar et al., 2020). PU has been demonstrated to exert a significant influence on technology acceptance in a wide range of research contexts.

Multiple studies underscored the theoretical significance of PU as a primary determinant of employee behavior in relation to the adoption and utilization of technological innovations. (Chuttur, 2009; Davis, 1989). These findings show that employees are more likely to adopt technology when they believe it directly contributes to better job outcomes, reinforcing that rational judgments about performance benefits drive acceptance. PU's consistent influence across numerous studies highlights its reliability and centrality in predicting user behavior. This also suggests that organizations seeking successful technology adoption must prioritize demonstrating clear value and performance benefits to users rather than focusing solely on technical functionality.

Replication Studies and PU. The foundational project undertaken by Schultz and Selvin (1975), later replicated by Robey (1979), demonstrated a strong correlation between PU, system utilization, and employee acceptance of technology. Building on these findings, Tornatzky and Klein (1982) performed a meta-analysis that reinforced the critical role of PU in the adoption of technological innovations among both organizations and employees (Chuttur, 2009). These studies collectively demonstrated that perceived usefulness was not just a theoretical construct, but a consistently observable predictor of real-world technology adoption. By showing that employees were more willing to use systems they believed improve their job performance, the research confirmed that PU directly influenced both attitudes and actual usage behavior. The meta-analysis by Tornatzky and Klein further strengthened this conclusion by proving that this relationship held true across different industries and organizational contexts, solidifying PU as a foundational element in technology acceptance research.

Bandura conducted further research in 1982 that highlighted the importance of PU and noted that behavior could be predicted by both self-efficacy and outcome judgements (Bandura,1982 ; Chuttur, 2009; Davis, 1989). Swanson (1982) also conducted research which concluded that PU was an important behavioral determinant and information quality was akin to PU. In 1985, Davis conducted further research on PU and concluded that employees would decide on whether or not to use a new system depending on PU, based on how well the technology or system would help them perform their jobs (Chuttur, 2009). Further studies conducted by Davis in 1989 and 2000 found that PU was the strongest predictor of user acceptance of new technologies. Similarly, a project conducted by Davis and Venkatesh in 2000 found that PU had a significant and direct impact on users' intention to adopt a new technology (Davis & Venkatesh, 2000). These studies collectively demonstrated that perceived usefulness was consistently the most powerful predictor of whether individuals chose to adopt a new technology. By linking

PU to self-efficacy, outcome expectations, and job performance, researchers like Bandura, Davis, and Venkatesh showed that users made rational decisions about technology based on its expected benefits. The repeated confirmation of PU across multiple decades and studies reinforced its central role in technology acceptance and underscored why it remained a core construct in TAM and later models such as TAM2 and UTAUT. The overall impact of PU was found to be a positive one. This meant, when users perceived that a technology was useful, they were more likely to adopt it (Chuttur,
2009; Mathieson, 1991). The studies that were conducted on TAM since 1975 found that PU significantly predicted users' or workers' intention to use a technology, which in turns led to actual adoption of the technology (Davis & Venkatesh, 1996). PU was found to influence users' attitudes towards a technology, therefore small businesses that focused on developing and promoting the usefulness of new accounting technologies were more likely to achieve higher adoption rates and experienced

improvements in their overall productivity and performance (Chuttur, 2009; Mathieson, 1991).

PU was one of the critical factors used to determine the intention to use a technology. This meant more workers were more likely to adopt a technology if they believed that it would be useful in their work (Davis, 1993; Mathieson, 1991). The greater the PU is, the more likely a worker would adopt the new technology introduced in the workplace. To increase PU, small business owners needed to clearly communicate the benefits of any new accounting technology to their employees (Davis & Venkatesh, 1996). For example, small business owners should communicate to their employees how the new accounting technology would help to automate repetitive tasks, reduced errors, and increased the speed of completing accounting tasks (Hooks et al., 2022; Lala et al., 2021; Vitro & Lopez, 2020).

Small business owners must clearly communicate and demonstrate the practical advantages of adopting new accounting technologies, particularly by showing how these systems saved time and resources, in order to help employees recognized their value. However, PU was subjective and could vary significantly among employees within the same organization (Chong et al., 2022). This variation occurred because a technology that one employee deemed as beneficial may not be regarded in the same way by another, even when used in the same work environment (Chong et al., 2022). Small business owners needed to illustrate the practical benefits of implementing new accounting technologies, particularly in demonstrating how these systems conserved time and resources, thereby helping employees to perceive their inherent value (Lala et al., 2021). The PU of any given technology was inherently subjective and differed across employees within the same organization (Chong et al., 2022). This was because a new technology that was perceived to be useful by one employee may not have been perceived in the same light as another employee (Chong et al., 2022). Small business owners needed to understand the specific needs requirements of each worker and customized any new accounting technology to meet their workers' needs (Uren & Edwards, 2023).

PEOU

PEOU was the second core construct of TAM and a major factor influencing whether employees accepted or rejected new technology. Davis (1989) defined PEOU as the degree to which a person believed that using a system would require minimal effort. Davis (1989) identified PEOU as the second and one of the most prevalent determinants that could influence workers to use or not to use a new technology. According to Davis (1989), PEOU referred to 'the degree to which a person believes that using a particular system would be free of effort', (p.320). PEOU is a major variable of TAM and was the deciding factor which could make a user feel the ease with which he or she could learn to use new technology to perform tasks (Holden & Karsh, 2010). If a technology was perceived to be difficult to learn, it was less likely to be accepted by the user, regardless of how useful that technology was (Dhingra & Mudgal, 2019). PEOU emphasized that even highly useful technology may be rejected if users found it difficult to learn or operate. This highlighted that successful technology adoption depended not only on functionality but also on reducing complexity and cognitive burden for users.

Davis (1989) emphasized that PEOU had been consistently validated as a critical factor in technology adoption through multiple research studies. Early scholars such as Tornatzky, Klein, and Bandura demonstrated that PEOU significantly influenced user behavior and decision-making regarding new technologies. Davis (1989) noted that several diverse lines of research have validated the importance of PEOU beginning with the meta-analysis of the 1982 project conducted by Tornatzky and Klein (1982) which highlighted the importance of PEOU in the adoption of technology or innovation. In 1982, Bandura noted the important role that PEOU played in predicting user behavior towards new technology. In his 1982 research Bandura supported the importance of
PEOU on self-efficacy, while highlighting that PEOU was similar to self-efficacy which Bandura (1982) defined as judgments of how well an employee could execute courses of action required to deal with perspective situations (Bandura,

1982). These findings showed that users were more likely to adopt technology when they felt confident in their ability to use it effectively and without excessive effort. This alignment between PEOU and self-efficacy underscored that technology acceptance was not only a technical decision but also a psychological one tied to confidence and perceived capability.

Replication Studies and PEOU. Research conducted by Swanson in 1982 provided evidence that PEOU was an important determinant of employee behavior towards acceptance or rejection of new technology(Aslam et al., 2023). In that project Swanson posited that workers would choose and use information reports based on the tradeoff between perceived information quality and the associated cost of accessing that information. Swanson theorized that the associated cost of access was similar to PEOU (Chuttur, 2009). Researchers have also shown that PEOU directly influenced PU, while both PEOU and PU influenced the attitude of the user towards technology (Chuttur, 2009, Davis, 1985). Davis (1985) noted a user's perception of the difficulty or ease that was required to use a system could directly affect the system usage behavior, which was the PEOU. If employees perceived that a new system was easy to use, then employees would display behavior that showed that they would more readily accept using that system, while if employees perceived the system to be difficult to use, they would display behavior to show that they rejected that system.

Attitudes

Attitude towards behavior was one of the main determinants of both TRA and TAM (Fishbein & Ajzen, 1975). Attitude towards behavior was defined by Fishbein and Ajzen (1975) as an individual's positive or negative feelings about working with the new technology. A worker's attitude towards a behavior was influenced by that person's belief about the behavior (Fishbein & Ajzen, 1975). Under TAM, Davis (1985) hypothesized that the attitude of a user toward a new technology was a significant indication as to whether the user would use or reject the technology (Chuttur, 2009). Meanwhile, Davis (1989) posited that the user's attitude was affected by two major factors, PEOU, and PU. Further research done on TAM showed that users' attitude would directly influence PEOU and PU (Kumar et al., 2020). However, it was possible for employees to display a negative attitude towards a system in the workplace, but the employee would still use the system because they believe that the system would be advantageous to their job performance (Davis, 1989).

Davis et al. (1989) posited that a user's attitude towards new technology was influenced by the user's relevant beliefs. When workers had a similar judgment about a particular outcome of a new technology, their beliefs about the outcome of the technology were typically consistent and directly related to their attitudes. Research have also shown that PU and PEOU have a positive effect on users' attitude towards technology (Christou, 2022).

Behavior

Davis (1989) noted that one of the constructs of TAM which was used to measure how users adopt new technology was users' behavioral intentions to use the new technology. Proponents of TRA, the antecedent of TAM, noted that users' beliefs influenced their attitudes towards new technology, which eventually affected those users' behavior towards the new technology (Christou, 2022). PU and PEOU have a strong impact on behavior and intentions, while a negative attitude towards new technologies decreases with time. Because of this argument, attitude was no longer viewed as a construct and by 1996 when Venkatesh and Davis analyzed the antecedents of PEOU, attitude was no longer included in the TAM (Kumar et al., 2020). This shift demonstrated that users' intentions to use technology were better predicted by their perceptions of usefulness and ease of use rather than by their general attitudes. As negative attitudes often declined over time with increased familiarity and experience, attitude became a weaker and less reliable predictor of actual technology use. Removing attitude from

TAM made the model more streamlined and empirically stronger by focusing on variables that consistently influenced user behavior, PU, PEOU, and behavioral intention.

Comparative Theories

Several conceptual theories were compared with TAM, two of which have been discussed in this project. They were the theory of reasoned action (TRA), and innovation diffusion theory (IDT). These theories provided a foundation for understanding the intricacies of the social and cognitive processes underlying the use and adoption of technology, and why users may or may not accept new technologies in the workplace outside of the two major external constructs of TAM, PU and PEOU.

Comparative Theories

TRA

TRA evolved from Dulany's (1968) theory of propositional control, a social psychological model which was first proposed by Martin Fishbein and Icek Ajzen in 1975 (Fishbein & Ajzen, 1975). TRA has been used as a conceptual framework to predict changes in human social behavior and is based on the premise that individuals make rational decisions about their behavior based on their attitudes and beliefs (Ajzen,

2012). According to the TRA model, an individual's intention to participate in a certain behavior was the most important determinant as to whether they will engage in that behavior (Ajzen, 2012). This framework highlighted that behavior was not random, but the result of deliberate reasoning based on beliefs and attitudes. By emphasizing behavioral intention as the strongest predictor of action, TRA established a foundation for later models like TAM that also link cognition to technology-related behavior. TRA's rational, decision-based view of human behavior helped shift research toward understanding internal motivations rather than just observable actions.

According to the TRA, an individual's behavioral intention is shaped primarily by their attitude toward the behavior and the subjective norms or social pressures surrounding it. The individual's intention was influenced by two main factors: the individual's attitude towards the behavior and subjective norms surrounding the behavior (Yoo, et al., 2021). While the individual's attitude encompassed the overall evaluation of the behavior in question, subjective norms referred to the perceived social pressure to engage in or avoid a particular behavior (Kacen & Gu, 2020,). Proponents of TRA recognized that individual's behavior was also influenced by factors beyond the individual's control, such as environmental constraints and availability of resources (Ajzen, 2012). Visual information such as simple charts, graphs, photographs, and sophisticated virtual environments were influential on users' attitudes and enhanced their decision-making (Kim et al., 2021). This means that human behavior is not only a result of personal beliefs but is also shaped by social expectations and external circumstances, such as available resources or constraints. Additionally, TRA implies that visual and contextual information can influence attitudes and decision-making, suggesting that users' choices are based on both internal evaluation and external persuasive cues. Together, these insights show that behavior is a rational process influenced by both personal assessment and the social environment.

Proponents of the TRA argued that users' perceptions of perceived usefulness

(PU) and ease of use were shaped by underlying psychological factors that influenced their interactions with new technologies.

According to TRA, users' attitudes, subjective norms, and perceived behavioral control determined their beliefs about an information technology's functionality and usability (Khechine & Brini, 2021). Studies conducted by TRA researchers showed that these psychological determinants significantly affected how users evaluated the usefulness and ease of use of new technologies and IT systems (Karahanna & Straub, 2020). These findings indicated that technology perceptions were not formed in isolation but were deeply rooted in social influence and personal control beliefs, which underscored the importance of considering behavioral and normative factors when predicting user acceptance. This perspective helped set the foundation for later technology-acceptance models by highlighting the psychological processes that shaped users' evaluations of technological systems.

The two main determinants of TRA are PU and ease of use which proposed that a user's beliefs about the functionality and usability of information technology (IT) are influenced by their attitudes, subjective norms, and perceived behavioral control

(Khechine & Brini, 2021). The results of studies conducted by proponents of TRA revealed that attitudes, subjective norms, and perceived behavior control significantly impact users' beliefs about the usefulness and the ease of use of new technologies and IT (Karahanna & Straub, 2020).

TAM and TRA share similarities. For example, both theories are focused on the relationship between attitudes, subjective norms, behavioral intentions, and both theories proposed that three factors are key determinants as to whether an individual would engage in a particular behavior (Ajzen, 2012; Karahanna & Straub, 2020). TAM focused on the adoption of technology, the two main key determinants of technology acceptance, PEOU and PU, and other external factors (Hooks et al., 2022). The TRA model could be applied to a wide range of behaviors, while TAM was specifically designed for technology acceptance (Ajzen, 2012, Vallerie et al., 2021). TRA focused on the individual's decision-making process, while the proponents of TAM took into consideration external factors such as social influence and system quality (Duffett & Papamichail, 2020;

Vitro & Lopez, 2020). Both TRA and TAM have been used extensively to predict and understand technology acceptance and adoption in the workplace (Chukkur, 2009). This comparison demonstrated that while both TRA and TAM emphasized the role of attitudes, norms, and behavioral intentions, TAM offered a more specialized framework by applying these principles directly to technology use. TRA explained behavior in a broad social context, but TAM expanded on it by incorporating external factors such as system quality and social influence to better predict technology adoption in organizations. As a result, TAM provided a more practical and contextspecific model for understanding how and why individuals accepted or rejected new technologies in the workplace.

Application to the Applied Business Problem

Small Businesses and AIS Evolution

The Accounting Information System (AIS) is integral to the operations of small businesses. AIS, which encompassed both accounting and information systems, is comprised the processes that facilitated the effective functioning and overall efficiency of the organization (Ibrahim, et al., 2020). The processes within the Accounting Information System (AIS) originated with data entry and concluded with the generation of financial statements and budgets utilized for forecasting (Ibrahim, et al., 2020). AIS assumed a vital role in small business operations by managing historical, current, and prospective financial data that affected both profitability and organizational growth.

Initially, AIS functioned as a supplementary mechanism focused on recording transactions. Traditionally, accountants relied on manual bookkeeping and physical documentation. However, with technological advancements, AIS transformed from a supportive function into an operational necessity for small businesses (Ibrahim, et al., 2020). Over the last four decades there has been significant development in the scopes and roles of AIS which have allowed for modern AIS to do more than capture and utilize historical and financial data. The use of computer technology in accounting started to become prominent in the 1950s which gave rise to accounting software (Banerjee &

Saraswat, 2022). Traditional AIS programs were developed and intended to be computerized versions of manual accounting processes. However, the early AIS could not support processes or satisfy the constantly changing needs of the various stakeholders. This led to a revolution in AIS which over time has become more sophisticated and improved the overall financial performance of the organization. The main functions of an AIS are listed in Table 2 which include collecting and storing data, providing information, providing controls, and providing forecasts for the future.

Table 2

Main Functions of an AIS

Functions	Explanation
Collect and store data	Systems collect and store data about business activities and transactions from source documents, record the transaction in the respective journal, then post the data to the appropriate ledger based on the account type.
Provide information	Information from the AIS is useful for decision making, used to generate financial and managerial reports.
Provide Controls	AIS utilize controls for the accurate processing and recording of data, while

	ensuring the data generated by the system is accurate and safeguards the business
Forecast of future	Some AIS can give forecasts for the future in the form of projected financial statements and budgets, allowing for analytical comparison with other firms and with different years for the firm.

Note. Created based on the main basic functions of AIS. Source (Christauskas & Miseviciene, 2012)

AIS and the Accounting Cycle

AIS has played a critical role in supporting the accounting cycle within small businesses. The AIS was responsible for processing every stage of the accounting cycle, beginning with the initial recording of transactions and continuing through the preparation of financial statements. Because it managed the full sequence of activities, the AIS needed to effectively support each component of the process. The accounting cycle referred to the series of steps a business undertook during each reporting period to record, classify, and summarize transactions, which were then used to generate accurate financial statements (Kimmel et al., 2020). This relationship suggested that the reliability and effectiveness of the AIS directly influenced the accuracy of financial reporting, making robust system support essential for small-business decision-making and compliance. By ensuring that each stage of the accounting cycle was handled properly, the AIS strengthened the overall financial management capabilities of small businesses.

In the accounting cycle, the AIS undertakes daily processes that affect the company's assets, liabilities, and the owner's equity. The accounting cycle of a business is important since the transactions involved are dependent on several factors such as the nature of the business, and the volume of information required by management. The AIS must be set up so that it will capture and record the appropriate accounting transactions or economic events as well as business processes. Figure 2 depicts the AIS.

Figure 2

Accounting Cycle

Note. From *Financial Accounting: Tools for Business Decision-Making*, by P. D.

Kimmel, J. J. Weygandt, and D. E. Kieso, 2020. John Wiley & Sons.

AIS and Business Process Management

Organizations had long conducted business by implementing a series of interconnected processes and activities designed to serve their consumers. This coordinated approach was only recently formalized under the term business process management (BPM). Trigo et al., (2016) noted that business processes (BP) were common to all businesses whether small or large and were referred to as strategic assets or 'the way things were done', or a 'complete, dynamically coordinated set of activities or logically related tasks that had to be undertaken to deliver value to customers or to fulfill strategic goals. Although traditional transaction-based AIS captured data that management used for financial reporting and decision making, AIS were not created to perform business process-oriented accounting, even though organizations have either implicitly or explicitly conducted business in the business process-oriented way. Over time, more sophisticated software were developed which captured the BPM of the organization (Trigo et al., 2016). These processes were particularly important to small businesses.

Small business owners were trying to streamline and formalize these processes since they became cognizant of this new way of thinking and were trying to incorporate BPM in AIS. The new AIS systems in the late 1990s and early 2000s were being designed with business process management suite (BPMS) capabilities (Trigo et al., 2016). Which meant this new type of AIS not only captured financial data but also took into consideration business processes, allowing small business owners to input control points as they deemed fit so they could collect and update decisionmakers with real time information.

Since the mid-2010s, AIS have been enhanced with advanced technologies that provided small business managers with integrated accounting and non-accounting information to support decision-making and the formulation of both short- and long-term strategic initiatives. Through the use of BPM software, small businesses were able to design, execute, and monitor a range of organizational processes to improve operational efficiency and effectiveness (Uren & Edwards, 2023). This demonstrated that AIS had evolved from simple record-keeping systems into strategic tools that supported managerial decision-making and organizational planning. By integrating BPM software, small businesses were not only able to automate processes but also gain real-time insights that improved efficiency and competitiveness. As a result, technology adoption became essential not just for financial accuracy but for long-term sustainability and strategic growth.

For example, cloud computing can be used to help with the promotion and adoption of BPMS in its software as a service (SaaS) based on the advantages of this technology. The result of this led to the new cloud computing service model known as, business process as a service (BPaaS; Lala et al., 2021). One of the key advantages of BPM that was used as a strategy by small businesses to remain competitive and profitable was that BPM technology adjusted the business processes based on changing market conditions requirements, which gave the small business management the opportunity to quickly and efficiently respond to changing market conditions.

This is directly applicable to my project because small business owners increasingly adopted cloud-based AIS that were integrated with BPM functions to improve efficiency and competitiveness. Cloud computing enabled AIS to operate as SaaS, and its evolution into BPaaS which has allowed small businesses to automate, monitor, and modify their financial and operational workflows in real time (Lala et al., 2021). Such integration supported the TAM, as it has enhanced PU by helping managers save time, reduce costs, and respond quickly to changing market conditions, particularly during crises such as the recent COVID-19 pandemic. It also reduced perceived effort because cloud-based systems required minimal installation, maintenance, or technical expertise. Therefore, BPM-enabled AIS not only contributed to operational efficiency but also aligned with the behavioral, organizational, and technological factors that influenced small business owners' decisions to adopt new technologies.

Adoption and Implementation Strategies for Accounting Software

Small businesses have had numerous effective strategies at their disposal which they have utilized to implement new or upgraded existing accounting technology so that their businesses can be competitive and profitable. Some of the adoption strategies available to small business owners included identifying the business needs, setting goals for the business, researching available software and comparing options, undertaking demo trials, consulting with vendors, planning for implementation of the new accounting software, identifying and involving key stakeholders in the business, timely data migration and clean-up, employee training and support, testing and evaluation of the new accounting software, monitoring and evaluating the performance of the new accounting software, keeping up to date with new accounting technology, seeking professional advice and doing constant follow up and revision after implementation (Bvuma & Marnewick, 2020). These strategies demonstrated that the adoption of accounting technology in small businesses was most successful when it was approached as a planned, collaborative, and iterative process rather than a purely technical upgrade. By assessing organizational needs, involving key stakeholders, engaging in vendor consultations and employee training, and continuously monitoring performance, small business owners were able to reduce resistance, increase perceived usefulness, and improve ease of use. This strategic approach aligned with the TAM, as it directly influenced behavioral intention and actual system use, ultimately contributing to profitability, sustainability, and competitive advantage.

Adoption Strategies

Numerous factors affected the adoption strategies of technology in an organization. Technological, environmental and organizational factors bore some type of influence on the adoption of accounting technology (Shahadat et al., 2023). Goal setting, software assessment, researching various software and software selection were some of the adoption strategies that are available to small business owners.

Goal Setting

The business owners must set clear and precise goals for the adoption of the accounting software for the organization. One of the main goals for the adoption of new accounting technology was that the AIS chosen for the business provided the small business owners with adequate financial and accounting information that benefitted the business (Douglas-Green, 2020; Marushchak et al., 2021). Goals for the adoption of the accounting software included some of, or all of the following, the time frame, the budgeted cost, the exact functions that the software is expected to fulfill, what vendor if any would provide the software or would it be a prepackaged software, the length of time that took for the allocation of training of existing staff and new hires, the timeline for the implementation and required support from the vendor after implementation, and the timeline to implement the software (Lala et al., 2021). A part of the adoption goal for the AIS was that the information generated was relevant, added value to the business processes while fulfilling the current and future accounting needs of the organization.

Needs Assessment

Small business owners must assess the specific accounting needs of their businesses which made it easier to select the new accounting technology. Prior to the adoption of any new AIS technology, firms had to be prudent in discerning which AIS was appropriate and useful to the specific needs of the firm (Lala et al., 2021). So, it was imperative for the business owners to assess the specific accounting needs of the business and the features they want the software to possess. The accounting technology chosen for the business must have the capacity to collect, store, retrieve, process, analyze, evaluate data, and transactions, while actually providing both the current and future financial image of the organization to the stakeholders (Lala et al., 2021). These strategies demonstrated that the adoption of accounting technology in small businesses was most successful when it was approached as a planned, collaborative, and iterative process rather than a purely technical upgrade. By assessing organizational needs, involving key stakeholders, engaging in vendor consultations and employee training, and continuously monitoring performance, small business owners were able to reduce resistance, increase perceived usefulness, and improve ease of use. This strategic approach aligned with TAM, as it directly influenced behavioral intention and actual system use, ultimately contributing to profitability, sustainability, and competitive advantage.

For example, depending on the nature of the business, the new accounting system might need to be integrated with several operational subsystems, including inventory management, warehouse management, order processing, customer invoicing, sales and production planning, supply chain coordination, and distribution functions. As suggested by TAM, managers needed to ensure that the new accounting technology addressed the operational needs of the business while also assessing employees' readiness to accept and use the system effectively (Lala et al., 2021).

The technological readiness of employees was an integral part of the needs assessment for new accounting technology for small businesses. Employees' technological readiness had a significant impact on their adoption or rejection of the new technology as explained by TAM (Uren & Edwards, 2023).The employees' attitudes towards new accounting technology in the business affected the successful implementation of any new technology, especially in the post COVID-19 era (Lala et al., 2021).The new accounting technology that was sourced for the small business should be tailored specifically to the type of small business and the processes that were needed for the daily operations of that specific small business.

Fordham and Hamilton (2019) conducted a project on 1,000 small businesses and found that of the 508 companies in the project that used computerized integrated accounting software packages, over 91 percent of the companies used software which were designed exclusively for their specific industry or line of business. To be more specific, the dry cleaners in the project used software designed for dry cleaning businesses while the dentists used software designed especially for their dental establishments. This project showed that it was beneficial to the business if a thorough research was conducted on the various types of software available on the market to determine which accounting technology would be best suited for the business. When the technology was specifically tailored to meet the needs of the organization, employees were more likely to accept it, and their attitudes and behaviors towards the technology reflected greater acceptance.

Researching and Selecting Available Accounting Software

Researching Available Accounting Software

Small business owners needed to research different accounting software products, their functions, and specific features in order to select the one that was best suited for their organizations. Small business owners also had the option of obtaining custom-made software. At the time of the project conducted by Fordham and Hamilton (2019), there were more than 150 well-defined and prepackaged software products available on the market; however, small business owners had to consider the various factors and functionalities of each software and how those features supported their organizational needs. (Banerjee & Saraswat, 2022; Marushchak et al., 2021). This showed that selecting an appropriate AIS was not a one-size-fits-all decision but required careful evaluation of software capabilities in relation to each firm's operational needs. By researching available options and comparing system features, small business owners increased the likelihood of adopting software that enhanced efficiency, accuracy, and decision-making. The availability of both prepackaged and customized solutions also demonstrated that flexibility in AIS selection was essential for aligning technology with business size, industry, and growth objectives.

In order for the research strategy to be successful, small business owners should establish a clear understanding of what the new accounting technology would achieve and align this with the organization's goals. In the post COVID-19 economy, business owners had to decide that type of accounting software was necessary to satisfy the accounting and managerial needs of their firms (Banerjee & Saraswat, 2022). As part of the research, it was necessary to determine the type of software; cloud-based or installed, and how the software would be installed, database.

The method of installing accounting software among small businesses was largely determined by cost, as many firms selected systems based primarily on affordability. The selection of the installation method was determined by cost as recent studies indicated that most small businesses chose their accounting software based on price (Banerjee & Saraswat, 2022). Although cloud-based software was more expensive to install than premise-based software, at the time of the project about 6 % of small and medium sized (SMEs) businesses used cloud-based of software for a number of reasons. First being portability, because in the post COVID-19 era a lot of small businesses elected to have their employees work remotely (Banerjee & Saraswat, 2022). This indicated that financial constraints played a significant role in technology adoption decisions, even when more advanced options such as cloud-based systems offered greater flexibility and functionality.

Although cloud solutions were initially more expensive, some SMEs still adopted them due to their portability and ability to support remote work in the post– COVID-19 environment. This demonstrated that perceived usefulness, convenience, and operational continuity could outweigh cost concerns when small business owners believed the technology would enhance resilience and productivity.

Selecting Accounting Software

The selection of accounting software was normally a complicated and critical business decision made by the company's management. Data have shown that for some small business owners the likelihood of selecting a particular accounting software was largely dependent on the cost of the software program (Hodgson & Ponte, 1991; Marushchak et al., 2021). Software selection based on cost has become a thing of the past because small businesses had the option of choosing free top-of-the-line accounting software such as Wave Accounting and Manager for their businesses and such software had sought after features (Yadav, 2022). However, small business owners still had to pay a fee for the 'free' software based on the features they selected to use.

In the early 1990s, researchers began examining the specific factors small businesses considered most important when selecting accounting software packages, two such researchers, Hodgson and Ponte conducted an in-depth project to ascertain what factors and features were the most important when it came to selecting software packages. Fifty-seven small businesses participated in the survey; 63 accounting packages were cited and no one package was dominant (Elikai et al., 2007). However, participants were asked to fill out the survey for each type of software used and 97 responses were tabulated (Elikai et al., 2007). Some of the accounting software packages that were identified and most frequently mentioned in that survey were QuickBooks,
Systems Application and Products (SAP), Oracle, PeopleSoft, Oracle, and Peachtree (Elikai et al., 2007). Some of the most important reasons cited for selecting the accounting software at that time were ease of use, flexibility, functionality, and

capability (Elikai et al., 2007). Small business owners would only be cognizant of the features of the software by comparing various software using criteria that are germane to organization.

Software Comparison

At this stage of the selection process, small business owners evaluated both the features and the nuanced functionalities of different software systems, along with their respective benefits. Historically, small business owners had exhibited a tendency to select software that yielded internal operational improvements while simultaneously enhancing their competitive advantage in the broader marketplace (Marushchak et al., 2021). Small businesses were able to select from various types of accounting software, including database-driven, installed, and cloud-based systems, while also determining whether to implement free or paid versions. According to *NerdWallet* (2024), some of the most highly rated free accounting software options included Zoho Books, Wave Accounting, ZipBooks, Odoo, BrightBooks, ProfitBooks, and Manager. This showed that free trials played a strategic role in reducing financial risk and uncertainty for small businesses during the software selection process. By experimenting with the software before purchase, business owners were able to assess functionality, usability, and compatibility with existing processes, which directly supported informed decision-making. Hands-on experience also increased employees' perceived ease of use (PEOU), making them more confident and willing to adopt the technology.

Small businesses owners or managers needed to compare the benefits of having installed or cloud-based software which was primarily based on internet connectivity. However, cloud-based accounting has become more popular with small businesses because it allows employees to work remotely in the post COVID-19 era as internet connections became faster and more modern. Small business owners were provided with various payment options to increase the affordability of accounting software, including one-time purchase fees and monthly subscription plans (Marushchak et al., 2021). Opting for software that included free trials or demonstrations was advantageous, as it enabled small businesses to assess the software's usability, features, and compatibility with organizational needs prior to purchase.

Demonstrations and Trials

A part of the software comparison was making use of free demonstrations and free trial periods of the products. Most software companies give a free trial period for testing their products (Marushchak et al., 2021). Small businesses made use of free trial periods and used the opportunity to learn as much about the software as possible because this reduced costs gave employees hands-on experience with the software. Business owners were encouraged to utilize the free trial period to determine how well the software functioned and whether it was a good fit for the organization (Marushchak et al., 2021). This showed that free trials played a strategic role in reducing financial risk and uncertainty for small businesses during the software selection process. By experimenting with the software before purchase, business owners were able to assess functionality, usability, and compatibility with existing processes, which directly supported informed decision-making. Hands-on experience also increased employees' perceived ease of use

(PEOU), making them more confident and willing to adopt the technology.

Proponents of TAM postulated that one of the ways to ensure that new technology was accepted by all users was to expose key stakeholders of the company to the technology at the initial design stages of a system. In this way, user suggestions could be taken into consideration to tailor the system and made it more functional for organization. It was at the demonstration stage that the key stakeholders got a firsthand look at how the PU and PEOU of the new technology affected their attitude towards the new technology (Venkatesh & Davis, 2000; Venkatesh & Davis, 2008). Also, free trials gave an indication of how much support the company might need from the vendor during and after the implementation process.

Vendor Consultations and Stakeholder Involvement

These were two crucial aspects of the software implementation process. Vendors of accounting software typically sold their products based on the advantages and features of the software (Marushchak et al., 2021). Small businesses were encouraged to negotiate for free updates, which helped reduce future costs associated with software maintenance and upgrades (Yadav, 2022). In addition, small business owners leveraged vendor consultations to ensure they received the necessary support and training for staff and other stakeholders who used the software during and after implementation.

Business owners used the implementation period to request software demonstrations and to test the accounting system within their actual business environments. Key organizational members participated in these demonstrations to determine whether the software met the functional requirements of their specific roles.

During this stage, stakeholders asked vendors targeted questions about how the system supported their individual job responsibilities. Software designers at the time also offered small businesses the option to purchase additional features or modules to expand system capabilities. Some vendors, such as

Intuit, the maker of QuickBooks, provided professionals who specialized in installing, integrating, and supporting the software within company systems, while others recommended third-party consultants for these services at an additional cost.

QuickBooks and Sage 50. These two accounting software programs represent the most widely adopted accounting software solutions among small businesses, primarily due to their cost-effectiveness and comprehensive features, which enabled small enterprises to enhance competitiveness and sustain profitability.

QuickBooks. In 2025, Quickbooks was the leading accounting software used by small businesses in the United States (Yadav, 2022). Data from 2022 revealed that approximately 26.56 million businesses in the United States used QuickBooks, while global users of the software totaled about 5.3 million (Yaqub, 2024). QuickBooks offered a range of advanced and intermediate features that made it the most popular software among small business owners, with an estimated 80% of small businesses in the United States.

QuickBooks features included memorizing transactions, loan program management, processing multiple reports, preventing prior-period changes, using custom data fields, batch invoicing, editing templates, remote access, stratifying reports, employing account numbers, managing fixed assets, attaching electronic documents, importing credit card transactions, providing data protection, and preparing letters and envelopes (Yaqub, 2024). QuickBooks is regarded as the leading accounting software because of additional attributes such as ease of use, flexibility, time-saving features, comprehensive reporting, affordability, security, and reliable customer support (Yaqub, 2024).

Sage 50. Sage 50 is also one of the leading accounting software programs in use. Launched in 1978 as a double-entry accounting system called Peachtree, it has had numerous feature updates, which now make Sage 50 one of the most preferred accounting software for small businesses (Miller, 2022). Some of the features of Sage 50 included advanced inventory management, job costing capabilities, human resources function, and shipping and logistics capabilities (Miller, 2022). In addition to the accounting functions, Sage 50 software included business operation features such as credit card processing options, tax, controlling expenses, check writing and tracking company returns and has an application that allow businesses can use to track customer complaints.

Implementation of the Accounting Software

Implementation of any accounting software has been a major feat for any organization. Jensen (2018) likened the implementation of new accounting software in a small business to a homeowner renovating his or her home. The homeowner must have an idea of what he or she wants the home to look like at the end of the renovation. However, the homeowner must take several steps before the renovation is completed. It is the same concept for small business owners, they must have an idea of what they want their overall accounting system to look like in terms of functions and end processes at the end of the implementation. The owners of the organization have several implementation strategies that they can follow.

Implementation Strategies

Implementation strategies for the accounting software should be well planned and coordinated. The successful implementation of an AIS was achieved by strategic coordination of strategy, organization processes, the actual technology and the stakeholders involved (Ibrahim et al., 2020). A successful implementation plan included a detailed project plan that outlined the implementation timeline, key milestones, and the parties responsible for various tasks. The plan for data migration from the old system to the new system while ensuring the integrity and accuracy of the organization's data was critical.

Thorough training and support sessions for all users were key at this stage. After which comes the pilot testing of the accounting software, then the software was first introduced on a small scale to test its functionality and resolved any issues that arose at that point. Proponents of TAM postulated that one of the ways to ensure users accepted a new technology was to expose users to the technology at the initial design stages of a system, where user suggestions could be taken into consideration to tailor the system and make it more functional for the users with requested features (Agarwal & Prasad, 1999). Consistent with TAM extensions, researchers emphasized the value of pilot testing to gather user input before introducing the full system across the organization (Venkatesh & Davis, 2000; Venkatesh & Bala, 2008). After the pilot phase ended, the finalized system could then be deployed organization-wide to promote higher levels of PU and PEOU.

After the pilot phase ended, the full system could be introduced to the entire organization. Continuous monitoring of the new software will be imperative for both the small business and the workers to ascertain any challenges and noted any barriers that might have arisen during and after the implementation phase, so that these can be addressed and corrected. **Challenges and Barriers in Implementing Accounting Software in Small Businesses** Implementing new accounting technology in small businesses had transformed financial management by enhancing efficiency, accuracy, and real-time access to financial data. However, small business owners often encountered several challenges and barriers throughout the adoption process. The primary challenges they faced included cost and financial constraints, data security and privacy concerns, project management difficulties, resistance to change among employees, insufficient training and technological skills, and complications associated with integrating new systems with existing processes (Phu et al., 2025).

Cost and Financial Concerns

One of the primary challenges small business owners faced when implementing new accounting technology was the cost. There were many costs to implement AIS, some of which were hidden, such as, the costs of the software, initial training and annual training of employees, customization of the software, redesigning of the software, and maintenance of the software (Ivanov & Petrova, 2024). According to a project conducted by the SBA, the cost of technology is a significant barrier for many small businesses, with 27% of small business owners citing financial constraints as a major impediment to adopting new technology (SBA, 2024). The price of the accounting software was one of the most important costs for small businesses. Some small businesses had small and limited budgets, and the cost of new technology could have easily caused budget overruns (SBA, 2024). In addition, small businesses could have experienced cost overruns stemming from high initial costs for purchasing software licenses, hardware and consulting services. The cost of accounting software ranged from several dollars to thousands of dollars, which was burdensome to small businesses with limited cash resources (Yaqub, 2022). Especially for those companies where the owners or mangers choses to use off-the-shelf software, that had to be customized, which was expensive and time consuming.

Small businesses also had to pay additional fees for licenses for the continual use of the software and for continuous software updates, maintenance and support long after the system had been implemented (Phu et al., 2025). So, while many small businesses were eager to enhance their services by implementing new accounting technology, many were hesitant to adopt such technology because of the financial costs and challenges. Another cost that small business owners had to undertake was the fee for hosting cloudbased software, since cloud-based accounting software had become quite prevalent since COVID-19, because more owners allowed their employees to start working remotely (Phu et al., 2025). The prevalence of new cloud-based accounting technology also gave rise to concern for the security of the company's data.

Security and Privacy Concerns

Data protection has become a major concern for small businesses, especially those using cloud computing software. One report found that 66% of small businesses had experienced a cyberattack, which highlighted the vulnerability of the sector (Ponemon Institute, 2019). With the adoption of digital accounting solutions, cybersecurity became a major concern. Small business owners were often targeted by cybercriminals due to their relatively weaker security infrastructures (Phu et al., 2025). Ensuring the protection of sensitive financial data through robust security measures became essential. In addition, new accounting software had vulnerabilities that could have been exploited by cybercriminals. Implementing new technology had to be accompanied by stringent security protocols to safeguard against breaches and complied with data protection regulations. Small businesses had to ensure that the new accounting system which had been implemented not only complied with data protection regulations but safeguarded the company's and clients' sensitive financial information.

Project Management

Delays in the implementation timeline occurred due to unforeseen issues leading to the project being extended. Another challenge experienced by small businesses was scope creep which occurred when uncontrolled changes arise, or the business leaders continuously expanded the implementation project leading to budget overruns and delays. The introduction of new accounting technology to a firm in stages was one of most costeffective ways to reduce project overrun and allowed the employees to adapt to a culture of change. In keeping with the TAM, small business owners were able to not only predict if the new system was being implemented and would be acceptable to employees, but these business owners were able to diagnose why a planned system would be unacceptable to employees and took corrective action to increase the acceptability of the new system in order to protect the company's investment in the new technology

(Marushchak et al., 2021).

Resistance to Change

Employees' resistance to change was a significant barrier or challenge faced by small business owners. A report done by McKinsey (2015) noted that change management was crucial when implementing new technology because about 70% of change programs undertaken in small businesses failed primarily due to employees' resistance and lack of management support. Employees who were accustomed to traditional accounting methods might have been reluctant to adapt to new technology. This resistance could have stemmed from fear of the unknown, concerns over job security, or simply a reluctance to alter established routines.

Employees may have resisted the new system because of their inability or failure to learn the new technology. Under the TAM, during the implementation, Davis (1989) posited that small business owners should be able to predict if the new system would be accepted by employees, diagnose why a planned system would be unacceptable to employees and took corrective actions to increase the acceptability of the new system in order to protect the company's investment in the new technology. The initial training for employees on the new technology was important, as well as continuous training as software updates became available.

Training and Skill Development

While the training of employees on new technology was costly, training was a critical step in the implementation process, and it was one of the challenges faced by small businesses with limited resources. The learning curve associated with the implementation of new software was steep, and inadequate training led to errors and decreased productivity (SBA, 2020). Ensuring that employees were proficient with the new system requires comprehensive training programs. Such training was tailored to existing employees, training on software updates, and training for new hires. One way to ensure extensive employees' acceptance of the new technology was to have employees test the pilot system, identified any problems or issues that they came across, and had those problems fixed before system implementation. Effectively incorporating employee feedback, improved the functionality of the software and the users' experience

(Marushchak et al., 2021.

Integration with Existing Systems

Ensuring the new software was compatible with other tools and systems used in the business was another challenge for small business owners. Gartner (2023) reported that integration difficulties with legacy systems remained one of the primary barriers to technology adoption in SMEs, with 35% of small firms identifying system integration as a major challenge. The International Data Corporation (IDC) indicated small businesses experienced difficulties in integrating new technologies with their existing systems, which has led to operational disruptions and data integrity issues. Small businesses often operated with a mix of legacy systems and manual processes. Integrating new accounting technology with these existing systems presented significant technical challenges. Compatibility issues also arose, requiring custom solutions or additional software to ensure seamless operation (Marnewick & Labuschagne, 2020). These integration hurdles demonstrated that adoption success depended not only on software features but also on the broader IT environment into which the system was deployed. Compatibility problems increased costs, delayed timelines, and introduced data-quality risks, which in turn reduced PU and PEOU among employees. Consequently, small businesses benefited when they invested in careful systems mapping, and phased rollouts to mitigate disruption and preserve confidence in the new AIS.

The Impact of New Accounting Software on the Profitability and Competitiveness of

Small Businesses

Enhanced Operational Efficiency

Operational efficiency was one of the primary benefits that small business owners expected to gain from implementing or updating their AIS. The economic and digital climate at the time of the project greatly influenced the need for small business owners to adopt new accounting software to ensure the success and competitive advantage of their businesses. The implementation of new accounting software significantly influenced the profitability and competitiveness of small businesses by improving the decision-making process, enhancing efficiency, and facilitating better financial management through the provision of more relevant and real-time data (Eniola & Entebang, 2023). This demonstrated that technology adoption was no longer optional for small businesses, but a strategic necessity driven by economic pressures and digital transformation. By improving operational efficiency, real-time access to financial data, and the accuracy of decision-making, accounting software directly contributed to profitability and competitive advantage. These outcomes reinforced the core premise of TAM, showing that when technology enhanced performance and reduced effort, small business owners were more likely to adopt and continue using it.

AIS not only reduced the time required to complete multiple tasks efficiently, but also minimized the risks of human error, ensured more accurate financial records, more timely financial reporting, reduction of costs, and allowed for the use of data analytics by small businesses (Al-Delawi & Ramo, 2020). Traditional accounting methods, which often involved manual data entry and paper-based processes, were time-consuming and susceptible to errors. AIS automated routine tasks such as bookkeeping, invoicing, and payroll processing, reducing human errors and shorter processing time of tedious and mundane tasks.

Such streamlining of processes enabled by accounting software allowed small business owners and their staff to focus on core business activities rather than spending excessive time on administrative tasks. This shift in focus led to increased productivity and better allocation of resources, which were crucial for maintaining a competitive edge in the market (Smith, 2025). As a result, small businesses that efficiently managed their finances responded more quickly to market opportunities and customer demands, thereby enhancing their competitiveness (Marnewick et al., 2020).

Improved Financial Decisions

Accounting software provided small business owners with valuable insights through advanced reporting and analytics tools. AIS allowed small businesses to analyze financial information at a faster speed and generated reports and critical forecasts essential for identifying trends, assessing risks and capitalizing on opportunities (Gelanis et al., 2018). AIS enabled the generation of detailed financial reports, which were essential for strategic planning and performance evaluation (Phu et al., 2025). By having access to real-time financial data, small business owners made informed decisions regarding pricing, inventory management, and investment opportunities.

AIS also allowed small businesses to utilize functions such as artificial intelligence (AI) to capture and analyze market trends, then capitalized on such trends to also make the businesses more profitable. In addition, new accounting software often included features for budgeting and financial planning which afforded small businesses the ability to create more accurate and realistic budgets, set financial goals, and monitor progress in real-time (Phu et al., 2025). Such a proactive approach to financial management assisted small business owners to navigate economic fluctuations and maintain financial stability, thereby contributing to long-term profitability. For example, a small business with robust financial planning capabilities avoided cash flow problems and ensured sufficient working capital to support growth initiatives, which was a significant cost saving measure.

Cost Saving and Profitability

Implementing new accounting software has led to significant cost savings for small businesses, which directly impacted the company's profitability. Studies have shown that the implementation of AIS in small businesses have allowed for such businesses to reduce the cost of operations, increased the profitability of the firms through increased productivity and contributed to the growth of said firms (Adebayo & Lamidi, 2021). This is owing to the fact that in most cases AIS reduced the need for extensive manual labor, allowing small businesses to reduce staffing costs by minimizing errors, streamlining BPM and reducing the costs associated with financial discrepancies and compliance issues (Adebayo & Lamidi, 2021). Such savings can be reinvested into the business to drive growth and innovation.

Another aspect of AIS cost savings was the reduction in expenses related to paper-based processes and physical storage. Digital record-keeping and cloud-based accounting solutions eliminated the need for large amounts of paper, printing, and storage space (Smith, 2025). This shift not only reduced operational costs but also contributed to environmental sustainability. Cloud-based accounting software offered secure and remote access to financial data, reducing the need for extensive IT infrastructure and associated maintenance costs which also increased the company's profitability (Phu et al.,

2025). AIS allowed efficient invoice and payment processing, which led to quicker collection and better cash flow management, which improved customer relations. One way that AIS contributed to the profitability of small businesses was through the enhanced security features and audit trails which helped to detect and prevent fraudulent activities (Phu et al., 2025). Improved internal controls and the ability to monitor such controls in real time reduced the risk of financial management, which l enhanced the company's profitability. **The Impact of COVID-19 on Small Businesses using New Accounting Technology** The COVID-19 pandemic profoundly impacted small businesses, necessitating rapid adoption of new accounting technologies to survive unprecedented challenges. COVID-19 challenges made small business owners focused on how new accounting technologies could facilitate resilience and growth amidst the crisis (Holl & Rama, 2024).

COVID-19 had both positive and negative impacts on small businesses.

Positive Impacts

Enhanced Financial Management and Resilience. The economic disruptions caused by the pandemic highlighted the need for robust financial management for small businesses. Owing to a reduction in demand caused by COVID-19, small businesses were unable to proportionally reduce their costs and remain profitable (Gao et al., 2023). With lockdowns, supply chain disruptions, and shifting consumer behaviors, accurate and realtime financial information became vital. AIS provides real-time financial data to assist small businesses monitor cash flow, track expenses, and make informed financial decisions swiftly, thereby enhancing financial resilience (Holl & Rama, 2024). The budgeting and forecasting tools provided by AIS were invaluable to small businesses and allowed them to plan and adjust their financial strategies amidst the fluctuating market conditions. The complete shutdown of the global economy gave rise to the need for small businesses to facilitate their employees working remotely wherever possible.

Facilitation of Remote Work. During the pandemic, the ability to access and analyze financial data remotely proved crucial for small businesses. New accounting technologies, particularly cloud-based solutions, enabled small businesses to maintain financial operations remotely, ensuring continuity despite physical restrictions (Papadopoulos et al., 2020). The prevalence of cloud-based AIS software enabled small businesses to continue their accounting operations remotely, which was crucial during the lockdowns and social distancing mandates. Employees were able to access financial data and perform accounting tasks from anywhere, which allowed for business continuity. COVID-19 caused a shift in the business model of small businesses with the use of virtual technologies and allowed access to improved financial data and analytics.

Improved Access to Financial Data and Analytics. Small business owners discovered the importance of financial data and data analytics. Akpan et al., (2020) posited that part of small businesses adjusting to the 'new normal' resulting from COVID-19 meant utilizing state-of-the-art technologies to digitize business activities and undertake virtual operations to enhance competitiveness, productivity, and business performance (Akpan et al., 2020). During the pandemic, the ability to access and analyze financial data remotely proved crucial for small businesses. Accounting software with advanced analytics and reporting capabilities offered detailed insights into financial performance and projections. This allowed small business owners to monitor their financial health closely and identify areas for cost reduction and revenue optimization (Holl & Rama, 2024). Furthermore, these technologies facilitated the preparation of accurate financial reports, required for securing emergency funding and government relief programs. By leveraging these tools, small businesses could navigate the financial uncertainties of the pandemic more effectively.

Streamlined Compliance and Regulatory Reporting. The pandemic also led to an increase in regulatory requirements and compliance obligations, especially concerning financial aid and support programs. New accounting technologies simplified the process of maintaining compliance by automating the generation of required financial documents and ensuring accurate record-keeping (Al-Okaily, 2024; Baig et al., 2020). This automation reduced the administrative burden on small business owners, allowing them to focus on strategic initiatives and operational adjustments needed to weather the crisis.

Cost Efficiency and Operational Continuity. Implementing new accounting technologies during the pandemic brought significant cost efficiencies. Automation of routine accounting tasks reduced the need for extensive manual labor, lowering operational costs and ensure business survival (Akpan et al., 2020). Additionally, cloudbased solutions eliminated the necessity for physical IT infrastructure, further reducing expenses (Phu et al.,). These cost savings were critical for small businesses facing reduced revenues and increased financial pressure. Moreover, the ability to access accounting systems remotely ensured operational continuity, enabling businesses to adapt to remote work models without compromising financial management.

Negative Impacts

Implementation Challenges. Small business owners that had not previously adopted new accounting technologies prior to COVID-19 faced challenges in transitioning during the pandemic. By the end of the pandemic about 75% of the populace indicated that they were using digital technologies because of the pandemic and they also indicated that they were intent on continuing the use of digital technologies when the economy returned to normal (Al-Okaily, 2024; Baig et al., 2020). During the pandemic, consumers were accessing digital services in historic proportions and businesses that were not equipped to offer customers services digitally did not survive and some went out of business (Al-Okaily, 2024; Baig et al., 2020). Small businesses required time, resources, and training to shift to operating digitally and these were hard to implement during the pandemic (Priyono & Moin, 2023). This demonstrated that the COVID-19 pandemic functioned as a catalyst for digital transformation, but it also exposed the vulnerability of small businesses that lacked technological readiness. Businesses that were already using accounting and digital technologies were more adaptable and resilient, while those without such systems struggled due to limited time, financial resources, and inadequate digital skills. The widespread shift to digital tools highlighted the importance of perceived usefulness and ease of use, reinforcing key constructs of the TAM as determinants of survival and post-pandemic continuity. Ultimately, technology adoption became not just an efficiency strategy, but a requirement for business continuity and competitiveness during and after the pandemic.

Cybersecurity Risks. During COVID-19, cybersecurity attacks became more prevalent. The rise in employees working remotely and their dependence on digital tools added to the increase in cybersecurity risks. Many small businesses which already had poor security infrastructure became vulnerable to cyberattacks. As a result, small businesses were forced to ensure the data privacy and protection of their companies and their customers data which proved challenging with dispersed workforce and increased online transactions (Alawida et al.,

2022). This demonstrated that digital adoption during the pandemic brought not only operational benefits but also heightened exposure to cybersecurity threats. Small businesses, many of which lacked strong security systems, were forced to rapidly improve data protection practices despite limited resources and remote work challenges. As a result, cybersecurity became a critical factor influencing technology implementation and trust in digital accounting systems.

Financial Constraints. The small businesses that invested in new accounting technology endured a significant burden, especially for those that were already struggling financially. The added cost of subscription fees, maintenance fees and the cost of new software compounded the financial constraints of many small businesses during a time when they were experiencing reduced revenues (Wahyuni, 2023). This showed that while adopting new accounting technology offered long-term operational benefits, it also placed immediate financial strain on small businesses with limited cash flow. For firms already facing declining revenues during the pandemic, the added costs of software subscriptions, maintenance, and upgrades made technology adoption a difficult and risky decision. As a result, financial pressure became a major barrier to digital transformation, even when the perceived usefulness of the technology was high.

How Implementing New Accounting Technology Can Help Small Businesses to Mitigate Risks and Avoid Business Failure

Small businesses during the period of the project operated in an environment marked by financial instability, inefficient operational processes, and increasing regulatory pressures. These challenges placed many firms at risk of failure. The adoption of new accounting technology played a critical role in reducing these risks by improving financial accuracy, enhancing operational efficiency, and supporting regulatory compliance (Sharma et al., 2023). This indicated that accounting technology functioned not only as a financial management tool but also as a safeguard for business continuity and sustainability. By reducing errors, increasing transparency, and providing real-time financial insights, technology adoption enhanced decision-making and helped prevent failures caused by mismanagement or non-compliance. As a result, technology became a strategic necessity rather than simply an administrative upgrade for small businesses.

Enhanced Financial Accuracy and Reporting

Traditional accounting methods were often prone to human error, leading to inaccuracies that allowed for serious financial repercussions. One of the primary benefits of implementing new accounting technology was the enhancement of financial accuracy and reporting (Adebayo & Lamidi, 2021). Small businesses that adopted cloud-based accounting software experienced significantly fewer errors in their financial reports (Phu et al., 2025). These technologies automated data entry and calculations ensured more accurate and timely financial information, which was crucial for making informed business decisions and maintaining financial health (Adebayo & Lamidi, 2021).These findings suggested that the adoption of modern accounting technologies not only reduced the risk of human error but also strengthened the reliability of financial reporting, which ultimately enhanced managerial decision-making and long-term business stability.

Improved Cash Flow Management

Improving cash flow was a critical strategy for small business owners seeking to prevent business failure. Effective cash flow management played a vital role in ensuring long-term sustainability, as cash flow challenges were identified as a leading contributor to small business closures (Al-Hattami &Kabra, 2024). The adoption of advanced accounting software enabled real-time monitoring of cash inflows and outflows, thereby enhancing financial decision-making. Programs such as QuickBooks facilitated the organization of accounting data and automatically generated cash flow statements, providing owners with timely insight into available funds for meeting operational expenses (Al-Hattami &Kabra, 2024). This demonstrated that small business survival depended not only on profitability but on the ability to maintain steady liquidity and meet short-term financial obligations. Poor cash flow management often caused otherwise viable businesses to fail, highlighting why many owners turned to accounting technologies that offered real-time monitoring, forecasting, and automated financial tracking. As a result, improving cash flow was not just a financial task but a strategic measure to ensure resilience and continuity.

Ensuring Compliance and Reducing Fraud

Adherence to financial regulations and reporting standards was a critical factor in preventing legal and financial repercussions for small businesses. The adoption of modern accounting technologies facilitated compliance by integrating automated features that ensured conformity with tax laws, accounting principles, and industry-specific requirements. Functions such as automated tax computations, electronic submission capabilities, and comprehensive audit trails enhanced regulatory compliance and minimized the likelihood of reporting errors. (Roszkowska, 2021). This demonstrated that accounting technology served not only as a financial management tool but also as a protective mechanism against legal and regulatory risks. By automating tax calculations, generating compliant financial reports, and maintaining accurate audit trails, these systems reduced human error and ensured greater accountability. As a result, technology adoption strengthened organizational credibility and helped small businesses avoid penalties, audits, and reputational damage

AIS enhanced security and reduced the risk of fraud. Advanced software solutions offered secure data storage, encryption, and accessed controls that protected sensitive financial information. By limiting access to authorized personnel and providing audit trails, these technologies help prevent fraudulent activities and ensure the integrity of financial data (Centobelli et al., 2022; Nguyen & Nguyen, 2022). This showed that the adoption of AIS was not only driven by efficiency and accuracy, but also by the need to safeguard financial information and strengthen organizational accountability. By incorporating encryption, controlled user access, and audit trails, these systems reduced opportunities for internal and external fraud, while increasing transparency and traceability of financial transactions. As a result, AIS contributed to building stakeholder trust and protecting small businesses from financial loss and reputational harm.

Enhancing Strategic Planning and Growth

The implementation of new accounting technology not only helped small businesses manage their finances more effectively but also supported strategic planning and growth. By providing accurate and timely financial data, these technologies enabled businesses to develop realistic budgets, set financial goals, and track their progress toward achieving them (Alsharari, 2022).This strategic approach to financial management helped businesses identify opportunities for growth and make informed investment decisions (AlQershi, 2021). In addition, modern accounting technologies were designed to integrate seamlessly with business management tools, including CRM and ERP systems. This integration provided a holistic view of business operations, facilitating better coordination and decision-making across different functions (Alsharari, 2022).

This showed that accounting technology played a strategic role beyond basic bookkeeping by enabling data-driven planning, performance monitoring, and long-term financial sustainability. With integrated systems such as CRM and ERP, small businesses were able to view financial and operational data collectively, which improved coordination, reduced inefficiencies, and enhanced strategic decision-making. As a result, technology adoption supported not only daily financial tasks but also broader organizational growth and competitiveness.

Implementing new accounting technology offered numerous benefits for small businesses, helped them mitigate risks and avoided business failure. By enhancing financial accuracy and efficiency, improving decision-making, ensuring compliance, reducing fraud, facilitating cash flow management, and supporting strategic planning, accounting technology played a crucial role in the success and sustainability of small businesses (AlQershi, 2021). As small business owners embraced these technological advancements, they achieved greater financial control, made informed decisions, and ultimately drove their businesses toward growth and profitability

(AlQershi, 2021). This demonstrated that accounting technology was not merely an operational tool but a strategic asset that strengthened business resilience. By improving accuracy, compliance, and financial visibility, it enabled small business owners to respond proactively to risks rather than react to crises. As a result, technology adoption contributed to long-term sustainability by enhancing control over finances, supporting informed decision-making, and improving the likelihood of business survival and growth.

Transition

In Section 2 of the project, I presented the conceptual framework and the exhaustive literature review. I discussed the conceptual framework of TAM and why it was appropriate framework to address the business problem, since the conceptual framework was the lens through which the project was grounded. In the literature review I explored the evolution of TAM, outlined three theories that compare with TAM and three theories that contrasted with TAM. I used the literature review to address the research question in the light of the TAM framework and presented information which addressed the business problem. Such information included implementation strategies for accounting technology, challenges and barriers in implementing accounting technology, the impact of new accounting software on the profitability of small businesses, and the impact of COVID-19 on new accounting technology.

In Section 3, I described the data collection process, which entailed data collection instruments, techniques, and a data analysis process, which outlined how to collect and analyze data, and validated and ensured the data collection instruments were reliable. In Section 3, I described the research method and design, the target population, sample size, and sampling methods.

While in Section 4, I presented the findings, application to professional practice, implications for social change or behavior, recommendations for actions, recommendations for further project and culminate with the researcher's reflections and a full analysis of the data collected using thematic analysis outlined by Braun and Clarke

(2006).

Section 3: Research Project Methodology

The use of accounting technology by small businesses has become a necessity (Lee & Runge, 2001). This qualitative pragmatic inquiry project was designed to ascertain what strategies some small business owners used to implement new accounting technology or software in their businesses to remain competitive and avoid business failure, especially in the post COVID-19 era. The participants in this qualitative pragmatic inquiry project were six small business owners in the southern United States.

The data collection technique that was used was conducting semi-structured interviews.

In Section 3, I describe the data collection process, which entails data collection instruments, techniques, and the data analysis process. I also describe the research method and design, the target population, sample size, and sampling methods. This section of the project includes (a) the role of the researcher, (b) participants, (c) research method and design, (d) population and sampling, (e) ethics research, (f) data collection instruments, (g) data collection technique, (h) data organization and technique, (i) data analysis, and (j) reliability, and (k) validity.

Project Ethics

One characteristic of qualitative research is that the researcher is the primary instrument for data collection and analysis (Lim, 2024). The role of the researcher is a multi-faceted one, encompassing many tasks and subtasks. Each of these roles demands a high level of commitment, rigor, and ethical consideration. Some of my roles as the researcher included observation, interacting with the participants while I conducted interviews, then later coding and analyzing the interviews using Nvivo 14 as verification of my Clarke and Braun's (2006) thematic analysis.

My role as the researcher began with identification of a research problem, formulation of the research question, and determining a methodological approach to address the business question. According to White and Ponto (2020), the importance of a well-conceived research design cannot be overstated, as it lays the foundation for the entire book. Researchers must conduct thorough literature reviews, using appropriate themes to situate their work within the existing body of knowledge, identifying gaps that their research will aim to fill in addition to considering the practical aspects of such tasks as data collection, meeting timelines, and allocating resources (Kiger & Varpio, 2020).

The ability to foresee potential challenges and devise strategies to mitigate such biases was another crucial role that I played as the researcher. A standardized interview protocol was used for each participant, which allowed for deeper insights and analysis and the collection of pertinent data (Yadav, 2022). The interview protocol for this project is in the appendix. Interviews are normally the primary way that researchers collect primary data in qualitative studies (Yadav, 2022). I conducted semistructured interviews for my project.

Qualitative researchers are focused on understanding how the participants interpret their experiences, engineer their worlds, and the meanings they attach to each experience (Belina, 2023). There is an emphasis on the need for meticulous data collection procedures to ensure the validity and reliability of the findings. Researchers must be adept at using various tools and techniques to gather accurate and meaningful data (Ghoston et al., 2020).

Normally, researchers have some type of experience or relationship with the project topic (Favetto et al., 2020). My relationship with this topic transcended a 30-year period of working in the field of accounting and being familiar with small businesses. My mother was a small business owner for many years, specifically in the restaurant industry. I performed various jobs as an accountant, ranging from basic entry-level accounts payable positions to serving as a federal auditor. During my tenure as a federal auditor and while pursuing a graduate degree in accounting, I discovered my passion for AIS, recognizing their variety and prevalence over the past three decades. I have worked with QuickBooks, Sage, and have also completed several online QuickBooks training courses with the aim of becoming a QuickBooks specialist and small business consultant in the future.

The Belmont Report

Ethical considerations are paramount during data collection, because qualitative research dictates that for valid and reliable studies, the investigation must be undertaken in an ethical manner (Larsson et al., 2023). One way the ethical practice in this project was enhanced was that, within an hour after conducting each interview, I wrote a threepart memo, one part of which addressed any personal biases in detail and any effects such biases might have had on the interview. The interview memo allowed me to think critically about my positionality and reflexivity, which were underlying concepts for conducting ethical and transparent research (Knott et al., 2022).

Additionally, the *Belmont Report* (1979) was used as a reference to gain a comprehensive and thorough understanding of the ethical guidelines and considerations that I needed to adhere to while conducting this research. Ethical research has a significant place in educational research, and the *Belmont Report* guiding principles were adhered to for this project (Brown et al., 2020). These principles ensure that research on human subjects is conducted in accordance with those principles (Nagai et al., 2023; Serpico, 2024). Researchers are responsible for ensuring that the research methodological strategies employed in the project aligned with the three ethical principles of respect for persons, beneficence, and justice (Campbell et al., 2021).

Respect for Persons

This principle of the *Belmont Report* includes ethical convictions of individuals getting treated as autonomous agents and the informed consent principle. Each participant was treated as an autonomous agent who was capable of making their own decisions, who was made aware of the nature of the research, the risks involved, and their rights to withdraw from the research at any time by sending an email, text message, or a telephone call requesting to do so. This meant that as the researcher, I treated all the participants who took part in the research fairly, in an ethical manner, as autonomous agents, respected their decisions, protected them from harm, secured their well-being, and got their informed consent.

Informed Consent. Qualitative and mixed-methods research that involve human subjects are required to undergo an ethics review and have an institutional review board (IRB) approval. One of the requirements of the Walden IRB included informing participants of this project about the topics to be discussed, the risks and benefits of participation, the manner and form in which data would be collected, and how participant confidentiality would be protected, any incentives for participating, and how the identity of the participants would be protected and kept confidential. All this information was included in what is called an informed consent form (Yadav, 2022).

As required by Walden University IRB, prior to participating in the project, each participant in this research was given a copy of the consent form that they signed, and each participant was given a copy for his or her records. The consent form included the following information: purpose of the project, procedures governing the project, the voluntary nature of the project, procedures for withdrawing from the project, risks and benefits of being a part of this project, privacy disclosure, disclosure of the interview as voluntary with no incentives or benefits offered, the rationale for selecting the participants, and the Walden University's IRB approval number for the project, approval no. 03-03-25-0138548 (Walden University Handbook, 2024). Such ethical vigilance was observed for maintaining the integrity of the research and upholding the trust of the academic community and research participants (Gefenas, et al., 2021).

Beneficence

The second principle of the *Belmont Report* involves the dedication of the researcher to protect the participants from any harm. In addition, all participants were treated in an ethical way by respecting their decisions and securing their well-being. The beneficence principle also required a detailed assessment of both the risks and benefits to the research to ensure that the welfare of each participant was prioritized (Nagai et al.,

2024).

Justice

This is the third principle of the *Belmont Report* and involves fairness in the project, who should bear the burdens of the research, and who should receive the benefits of the research. Under the principle of justice, the selection of the research participants was done in a manner that avoided the exploitation of vulnerable populations so that no particular group was unfairly targeted or burdened with risky research. The researcher was responsible for ensuring that the participants who bore the risks of the research were the ones who benefitted from the findings of the research (Serpico, 2024).

There was no incentive for participating in the project. All participants' information was kept confidential, and the interviews recording are being kept in a safe, and the researcher is the only person with a key to access the data. Any information provided by the participants during the interview have been kept strictly confidential. None of the participants names or identifiable information will be shared or sold. In addition, any other personal information or trade secrets that were divulged

will not be revealed or shared with anyone. As the researcher, I ensured the participants' anonymity. To do this, I gave each participant a code, for example P1, P2, P3, which was used to replace the participant's name and company information to maintain each participant's privacy in all stages of the research (Silverio et al., 2022). All the participants' names, company names and any identifying details has been excluded from all the reports. The research data will be kept securely in a safe for a period of at least 5 years to protect each participants' confidentiality, as required by Walden University. After 5 years all the participants' data will be destroyed in a safe manner with a shredder (Walden IRB
Manual, 2024).

Nature of the Project

Research Method

Choosing the best-suited research methodology for the project will ensure successful research strategies (Reed et al., 2021). The qualitative research methodology was selected for this project because it allowed me to explore and analyze participants' lived experiences and opinions as well as understand the participants' values and preferences for selecting a particular accounting technology for their small business (Youn et al., 2021). My research aim, analysis, objective, specific research question, appropriate mode of engagement and conceptual theory all helped to determine the research methodology chosen.

The qualitative research methodology aligned with my research question because it allowed me to get the subjective and nuanced feelings, opinions, and perspectives of small business owners and managers. Since the qualitative research incorporated an interpretive naturalistic approach, I was able to interview and observed the participants in their natural settings (Thunberg & Arnell, 2022). Qualitative researchers conduct interviews using open-ended questions to generate themes, capture participants' experiences and perceptions of their reality so providing answers to the research questions (Yadav, 2022).

Research Design

Just as it was important to select the appropriate research methodology, it was also important to choose the correct research design. I refrained from selecting a design based solely on familiarity or comfort. Instead, the research design was selected based on its appropriateness and ability to best address the research question (Yadav, 2022). For this project, a pragmatic inquiry design was employed, as it was deemed most suitable for practical research by integrating multiple perspectives and balancing deductive and inductive reasoning in addressing the business problem (Ramanadhan et al., 2021). Utilizing the pragmatic inquiry allows the researcher to focus on solving real world problems by integrating theory and practice since the researcher applied practical knowledge to address the research question (Allemang et al., 2022).

Population, Sampling, and Participants

Population

The population is the complete set of individuals, events, or objects that exhibit the behaviors and/or possess the characteristics of interest to the researcher (O'Sullivan et al., 2021). For this project, the population consisted of the 1,113 small business owners in the Clarksville, Tennessee (Clarksville, Tennessee Business Directory). The target population is a more specific subset of the population that the project was geared towards, which in this case was the small business owners who have implemented new accounting software or have upgraded their existing accounting software since COVID19. Yaqub (2024) noted that about 64.4% of small businesses make use of accounting software which is equated to approximately 716 small businesses in Clarksville, TN. The expected sample was six small business owners or managers from the target population who had implemented new accounting software or had upgraded their existing accounting software since COVID-19.

Sampling

The sample size and selection methods should be carefully selected to ensure the results of the project are credible and transferable, so the proper sampling technique for the research at hand should be chosen (Guest et al., 2020). For this project the sample size was six small businesses owners in the Clarksville, Tennessee area, who have implemented new accounting software or have upgraded their accounting software in their businesses. The sample size in any qualitative project should not be predetermined and should be large enough to allow for data saturation. In the meantime, the researcher also ensured that the sample size was appropriate for the type of project (Bendt, 2020). The sample size for a qualitative pragmatic inquiry project is six participants not just for statistical prowess but to achieve data saturation (Bendt, 2020; Yadav, 2022).

Data saturation occurs when no new themes or insights are observed in the data, indicating that the sample size is sufficient to capture the variability in the population, and can be achieved with a sample size as small as five to six participants (Fusch & Ness, 2015). A sample size of six small business owners was sufficient to achieve data saturation for my project and allowed me to capture the variability in the small business population in this city.

Merriam and Tisdell (2016) noted that there is no definitive answer to the number of participants that should be in a sample, but the researcher should instead focus on the questions being asked, the data being gathered, the analysis in progress, the resources that are available to support the project, and sampling until data saturation or redundancy is reached. One of the main goals of the sampling method chosen was to ensure information richness, which means the data collected from the sample provided in-depth information about the research question.

Proponents of the qualitative pragmatic inquiry design posited that a sample of six small business owners should be able to provide rich data for this project. Also, a sample size of six was appropriate for this project because the goal was to conduct an in-depth exploration of the implementation of accounting software phenomenon in small businesses, which was a very focused context, while keeping in mind complexity of the research question, and the methodology that was used.

There are two types of basic sampling used to conduct research, probability and non-probability sampling. Since generalization based on statistics is not a goal of qualitative research, probability sampling was not justified for qualitative research, nonprobability sampling was the best sampling method for most qualitative research (Bendt, 2020). Again, the sample for this project was six small business owners or managers taken from the target population who implemented new accounting software or had upgraded their existing accounting software since COVID-19.

Since I needed the six small business owners to have implemented new accounting technology , I used both convenience and purposeful sampling techniques to select the expected sample. Both convenience and purposeful sampling are nonprobability sampling methods that I used to determine what small businesses would be included in the sample based on certain criteria (Thomas, 2022). There were several types of purposeful sampling available to me and based on the nature of the research I chose the criterion-based selection type for this research. Within criterion-based purposeful sampling, the researcher initially established the essential attributes of participants relevant to the project and selected business owners whose enterprises fulfilled those predetermined criteria (Wolff et al., 2020). To begin purposeful sampling, I first determined what selection criteria were to be used to select the participants in the sample size. For this project, the two criteria that were required to participate in this project were: (a) be a small business owner in Clarksville, Tennessee and, (b) the business owner must have implemented new accounting software or upgrade existing accounting software.

A pre-screening survey was conducted by contacting small businesses within the target area. Following an introduction, the researcher posed three key questions to determine eligibility: (1) Are you a small business owner?, (2) Have you implemented or upgraded accounting software in your business?, and (3) Are you willing to participate in this research project? Businesses that responded affirmatively to all three questions were included in the participant pool.

I scheduled a time to meet in person and went over the details of the project, and what the project entailed. At the meeting, I went over the consent form, gave the participants a copy of the interview questions, went over the Walden IRB requirements for this research, and scheduled the actual interview for each participant.

Participants

The participants for this project were six small businesses in the Clarksville, Tennessee, business community which represented the project sample. The criteria for participating in the project included (a) be the owner/operator/manager of a small business in the Clarksville, TN area, (b) the owner/operator/manager had implemented new accounting software/technology or had upgraded exiting accounting software or technology since COVID-19.

I secured permission to undertake the research from the business owners or appointed party, as well as from Walden University Institutional Review Board (IRB). I secured the necessary permission from the small business owners. I gained access to the participants by accessing the names and addresses of all the small businesses in the Clarksville, Tennessee area from the local Chamber of Commerce or through the Office of the Secretary of State (Godolphin et al., 2023). If the participants were located in remote sections of Clarksville, I had planned on using some of the strategies highlighted by Kaufmann and Tzanetakis (2020), such as sending emails, letters or in-person visit to get access to them.

After making initial contact with the small business owners, I emailed letters of invitation to all the participants detailing the objectives of the project, a description of the confidentiality and informed consent process and my contact details were also included in that invitation. Each participant signed an informed consent form indicating their willingness to participate in the project. This form was signed before I conducted each interview. After receiving the signed consent forms, I then set up interview times and dates for each participant based on their schedules. I ensured that I had a good working relationship with the participants so I could fulfill the obligations of the research.

The Belmont Report's principle of fairness for all participants was adhered to by making sure all the participants in the project met the criteria necessary for the research. I practiced bias management and ensured that I was mindful of possible biases at all stages of the research. I took deliberate steps to mitigate all biases, which included the data analysis stage of the research. For example, during the interview process, I reduced nonverbal expressions to prevent bias.

To ensure data saturation, I conducted the interviews and follow-up with each participant until data saturation was reached (Fusch & Ness, 2015). Data saturation refers to the point in data collection when no new information or themes are emerging from the data (Mwita, 2022).

Data Collection Activities

Data Collection Instruments

In qualitative research, data collection is about asking, watching and reviewing all data collection steps undertaken by the researcher who is the primary instrument for data collection and analysis (Merriam & Tisdell, 2016). There are different types of data collection instruments, such as observation, interviews, and questionnaires, and the researcher chose to use the most appropriate one for the research so that rich data was collected (Taherdoost, 2021). This approach underscored the importance of aligning data collection methods with the study's purpose, as the appropriateness of the instrument directly influenced the depth, credibility, and overall quality of the findings.

For this qualitative pragmatic inquiry project, the data collection instruments were the researcher conducting semistructured interviews. Taherdoost (2021) opined that prior to deciding on the data collection method, the researcher should decide on what type of data is required for the project. Interviewing is one of the most popular forms of data collection in qualitative studies and in some cases, it is the only means by which data is collected (Taherdoost, 2021). The interview questions can be found in Appendix B.

I conducted semistructured interviews. A research interview should not just be a spontaneous exchange, but it should be a structured and purposeful conversation (Merriam & Tisdell, 2016). A semistructured interview is one in which the questions and the order in which the questions are asked are decided on prior to the interview, since specific information is required from the participants (Merriam & Tisdale, 2016). In the semistructured interviews I used follow-up probing questions which allowed for flexibility. Some of the benefits of using a standardized face-to-face interview are that the participants will have the opportunity to get clarification on any questions they do not understand, there is a high response rate for this type of interview, and the researcher will be able to obtain rich data which will ensure data saturation (Taherdoost, 2021).

I used an interview protocol for this project (Appendix A). The interview protocol is a list of the interview questions and procedures that I followed during the interviews. In addition, the interview protocol included my script prior to the start of the interview, script for what was said after the interview, and prompts to collect the informed consent form. For example, some researchers have been known to forget such steps as turning on the recording device prior to the start of the interview and missing out on collecting rich data (Johnson et al., 2023). Dunwoodie et al. (2023) opined that the interview protocol adds to the quality and consistency of data collection instruments by providing structure for the researcher. The rationale for employing an interview protocol was diverse and multifaceted, as conducting interviews could be particularly challenging for the researcher. Using an interview protocol ensured that the participants answered the research questions regarding complex constructs in a thoughtful manner.

Transcript Review

The researcher will enhance the reliability and validity of the data collection instruments and process by conducting transcript review. Stahl and King (2020) noted that research participants are often provided with a pre-publication copy of the research write-ups to solicit their feedback regarding the accuracy of the data. This technique is referred to as member checking, and it is another way to add to the credibility of the research. In this case, transcript review was used to verify validity, accuracy, credibility, and transferability of the collected data.

The interview protocol also included steps on how the researcher needed to conduct transcript review by explaining to the participant that I transcribed the data from the interview and gave the interview participants the opportunity to confirm or deny the data collected from the interview right before the follow-up interview was conducted.

The interview protocol can be found in Appendix A.

Data Collection Techniques

Researchers have multiple data collection techniques at their disposal when working with qualitative data. Such data collection techniques include questionnaires, observation, interviews, physical visits, and data collection (Merriam & Tisdale, 2016). The data collection techniques for this project were face-to-face semistructured interviews. "The data collection techniques used, as well as the specific information considered to be data in the project, are determined by the researcher's theoretical orientation, by the problem and purpose of the project, and by the sample selected" (Merriam & Tisdell, 2016, p. 106). The use of multiple data collection techniques in qualitative research not only allows the researcher to gather data from various perspectives and enhance the validity of the research, but it allows for the triangulation of research data (Taherdoost, 2021).

For this research, I used semistructured face-to-face interviews, which were taperecorded, and I also followed the interview protocol. The interview was conducted at a time and place convenient for the participants. Also, I ensured that the interviews were undertaken in a spaces with minimal background noise, no distractions and places where both the participant and researcher felt relaxed (Knott et al., 2022). Before the interview commenced, the researcher provided a list of the questions (see Appendix B) as well as 2 copies of the proposed consent form.

A part of the data collection technique was how the researcher mitigates biases, called observer bias (Larsson et al., 2023). In qualitative research, the researcher's bias can influence the project. There were several strategies I used to mitigate research bias thereby ensuring the credibility and trustworthiness of the project. These strategies that were available to the researcher included but were not limited to bracketing, reflexivity, and the use of a codebook to mitigate bias (Knott et al., 2022).

Bracketing

Bracketing is a strategy which has its roots in phenomenological research and involves the researcher consciously identifying and setting aside his or her preconceptions and assumptions about the research topic (McLeod, 2024). The researcher engages in reflective self-examination, recognizing and identifying personal experiences and biases he or she has brought to the research process (McLeod, 2024). This technique of bracketing allows the researcher to approach data collection and analysis with an open mind. In practice, bracketing involved the use of reflective journals or memos where researchers documented their assumptions and preconceived ideas before and throughout the research process (Chan et al., 2021). For example, I had planned on making descriptive field notes, before and after each interview and I annotated my feelings, attitudes, and such innuendoes as the participants' gestures that went on during the interview, but I was unable to do so because of time constraints, I was only able to make notes for one of the interviews.

Reflexivity

Reflexivity was an ongoing process of self-examination that I undertook to reflect on how my background, beliefs, and actions influenced the research process. Proponents of reflexivity acknowledge that biases cannot be fully eliminated, but they can be addressed and managed in a transparent manner, such as the researcher continuously doing self-critique about his or her own biases, preferences, values, and preconceived ideas regarding the phenomenon during the entire research process (Renjith et al., 2021). Reflexivity adds to the transparency of the research process while strengthening the credibility of the research which was not conducted in a single session, but it was a continuous process (Olmos-Vega et al., 2023). Reflexive practices included maintaining a reflexive journal where researchers documented their evolving thoughts, feelings, and reactions throughout the research process. (Olmos-Vega et al., 2023). I was not able to keep a reflexive journal owing to time constraints.

Codebook

A well-constructed codebook provides detailed definitions and guidelines for coding categories, which reduces interpretive bias and increases the reliability of the findings (Castleberry & Nolen, 2022). A codebook is a structured research tool which allows the researcher to add another level of transparency and consistency to the data analysis process. The researcher defines the codes, providing a description for each code, and offers examples to clarify how each code should be applied. This coding procedure ensures that similar data is consistently coded throughout the research (Namey, 2021). The data were coded through a systematic, multi-stage qualitative analysis process supported by NVivo software to ensure organization, accuracy, and rigor. I began with open coding by uploading all transcripts into NVivo and reviewing them multiple times to identify meaningful statements and assign initial codes. NVivo allowed me to label, categorize, and track emerging concepts efficiently. I then conducted axial coding to organize related codes into broader categories that reflected patterns across participant responses. Finally, I completed selective coding to refine these categories into overarching themes aligned with the study's research questions. Throughout the process,

NVivo's memo features and query functions helped me maintain consistent coding decisions and engage in constant comparison. Using NVivo strengthened the analytical process by improving the accuracy of code management, enhancing transparency, and supporting the development of themes that were grounded in the data. By applying a rigorous coding structure and leveraging NVivo for organization and verification, the study ensured that the resulting themes accurately represented participants' perspectives and supported trustworthy qualitative findings.

Interview Questions

1. What effective strategies did you use to implement new accounting software to remain competitive?
2. How did you measure the effectiveness of the strategies?
3. What challenges did you encounter when implementing the strategies?
4. How did you overcome the challenges?
5. What challenges to adopting the new software did you encounter?
6. How did you overcome those challenges"
7. What effective strategies did you use to avoid business failure?
8. How did you measure the effectiveness of the strategies?
9. What challenges did you encounter when implementing the strategies?
10. How did you overcome the challenges?

Data Organization and Analysis Techniques

Data Organization Techniques

Data organization techniques encompass data management systems which were important for keeping track data, making it easy for me to reference and access the data collected for present and future use. Some of the systems that could have been used for tracking included research logs, reflective journals, cataloging, and labeling systems. Such data collection techniques could have assisted the researcher with systematic data analysis (Taherdoost, 2021).

For this research project, I kept track of data in a systematic way. Each participant was given a code to conceal their identity. Since no identifying information was used for any of the participants. I recorded each participant's interview with a recorder, and the tapes were labeled with each participant's code. All notes, including field notes and transcribed data, were labeled with the participant's code. I ensured that I understood how to create codes and themes following the verbatim transcription of the interview data. I did this by researching the topic and learning how to use the most up to date technology available, Nvivo 14. Transcription represented a critical step in the process of data organization. Although computer-assisted transcription software was utilized, the researcher carefully reviewed and corrected transcripts to address any unanticipated errors or omissions (Jenkins et al., 2021).

Research logs and research journals were used in this research. Research logs were systematic records of the progress of the research that included data and time entries, detailed descriptions of the research activities, recording observations, results, and preliminary conclusions (Zhaoxue et al., 2021). I did not use a reflection journal because of time constraints.

Data Analysis

Data analysis is a complex and mysterious portion of a qualitative project (Kiger & Varpio, 2020). The qualitative component of the project provided a clear description of the data analysis methods employed. To strengthen the project's validity, I ensured transparency by detailing how the analysis was conducted and how the findings were interpreted (Taherdoost, 2021).

Thematic Analysis

The data collected were analyzed using thematic analysis methods. Thematic analysis is a practical data analysis approach for analyzing qualitative data which includes querying a data set to identify and analyze patterns among the data set (Braun & Clarke, 2021). Thematic analysis in this research involved the interpretation and description of data to select codes and construct themes. Thematic analysis is flexible and can be used with any theoretical framework, as well varying range of project questions, research designs, and sample sizes (Braun & Clarke, 2021). Thematic analysis is a versatile method which can also be used to understand experiences, thoughts, or behaviors across a dataset (Kiger & Varpio, 2020).

Braun and Clarke (2021) opined that thematic analysis is versatile, as it acts as the foundation for other qualitative research methods, or it can be stand alone as an analytic method. Thematic analysis was used to show how a certain social construct started, and it allowed me to search for more latent, deeper themes within the data. In addition, thematic analysis allows the researcher to engage in emancipatory investigations and sought to ascertain the social meanings and implications behind the research question (Braun & Clarke, 2022; Kiger & Varpio, 2020).

Researchers need highly structured analytical guidelines and should be cognizant of several overriding principles to press for high quality analysis (Taherdoost, 2021). In this research, the sequential process was used for data analysis was the six-phases of data analysis postulated by Braun and Clarke (2006), which were, (a) familiarizing yourself with the data, (b) generating initial codes, (c) search for themes, (d) review themes, (e) define and name the themes, and (f) producing the report or in my case writing up the findings (Braun & Clarke, 2006; Kiger & Varpio, 2020).

Phase 1: Familiarizing Yourself with the Data

Kiger and Varpio (2020) noted that at in this stage of the data analysis process, the researcher became familiar with the entire data set. Braun and Clarke (2006) opined that the researcher should immerse his or herself in the data, so much so that they became aware of the depth and breadth of the content of the data. This meant that I actively and repeatedly read through data set, searched for meanings and patterns and became familiar with all aspects of the data. At this beginning stage of the analysis, the researcher should refrain from coding the data or searching for themes (Kiger & Varpio, 2020). Instead, I made notes and annotated ideas for coding for the other steps in the data analysis.

Phase 2: Generating Initial Codes

After the researcher becomes familiar with the data, they take notes and compile an annotated initial list of codes based on the data, then the researcher produces initial codes from the data (Braun & Clarke, 2006; Braun & Clarke, 2023). The researcher recognizes that this stage of the data analysis process produces initial codes, not themes (Kiger & Varpio, 2020). In Stage 2, I generated initial codes by systematically reviewing each transcript and identifying meaningful segments of data. After becoming familiar with the content, I used NVivo to highlight relevant excerpts and assign descriptive labels that captured the essence of each data segment. I coded inclusively, ensuring that all data relevant to the research questions were captured, even if certain ideas overlapped across participants. During this stage, I focused solely on producing initial codes rather than developing themes, consistent with Braun and Clarke's guidance that codes serve as the foundational building blocks for later theme development. I also kept analytic memos to document coding decisions and maintain consistency throughout the process.

A code is the most basic element of the raw data that can be assessed in a meaningful way regarding the phenomenon which the researcher deems interesting (Braun & Clarke, 2006; Braun & Clarke, 2023). A code can be semantic, addressing explicit or surface meanings of data items, or a code can be latent and addresses deeper underlying meanings or assumptions (Kiger & Varpio, 2020. The codes that were generated in this phase were well-defined and did not overlap with other codes. Coding was conducted both manually and through the use of Nvivo 14. I coded the data by tagging and naming selections of text within each data item.

After the codes were identified, I aligned each code with representative data extracts and verified that all pertinent excerpts had been appropriately coded. According to Braun and Clarke (2006), the researcher may have needed to copy data extracts from individual transcripts or reproduce printed excerpts. Subsequently, each code was organized and collated into separate files.

Clarke and Braun (2006) highlighted a number of key steps that the researcher needed to follow in the second phase of data analysis, (a) code as many themes and potential themes as possible, as some items might prove to be interesting later on in the analysis, (b) keep some of the data surrounding the code if relevant, to prevent losing context because of the coding, (c) individual extracts of data can be coded in as many themes as the researcher deem fit, and (d) the data set will have some form of contradiction, but a thematic map will produce data patterns and relationships.

Phase 3: Searching for Themes

In this phase of the analysis, the codes from phase 2 were organized into themes. A theme is a patterned response (Kiger & Varpio, 2020). Braun and Clarke (2012) explained that if data analysis were likened to constructing a house, the individual codes would represent the bricks and tiles, while the themes would form the walls and roof. The process of building those walls and roof, developing themes from coded data, was both active and interpretive in nature (Kiger & Varpio, 2020).After the data was initially coded and collated, I had a long list of different codes from the data set. Then the researcher attempts to sort the different codes into potential themes. The researcher also tries to ascertain how different codes could be combined to form an encompassing theme (Braun & Clarke, 2006; Braun & Clarke, 2023).

In this phase I used illustrations such as tables to categorize the different codes into themes. Braun and Clarke (2023) suggested that the researcher should write the name of each code, the description of each code on pieces of paper, and then take the time to organize each code into themes-piles. The researcher should start to think of the relationship between the various codes, themes, and between different levels of themes to identify themes and sub-themes. Some themes might not fall into any category and should be labeled as miscellaneous and used to accommodate those themes which do not fit into the main themes.

In Stage 3, I examined the initial codes and organized them into potential themes by identifying patterns, relationships, and areas of conceptual overlap. Using NVivo, I grouped related codes into broader clusters that captured meaningful aspects of the participants' experiences. During this stage, I focused on how different codes combined to represent larger ideas relevant to the research questions. I developed preliminary thematic maps to visualize how codes connected across the data set.

Phase 4: Reviewing Themes

This phase of the data analysis was a two-step process. Kiger and Varpio (2020) noted that in the first level, the researcher examines the coded data with each theme to ensure that a suitable fit and asked a series of questions, (a) did each theme have adequate supporting data? (b) were some themes too large or diverse? In addition, the researcher ensures that the data within in theme is consistent and has adequate commonality and could still be separated from other themes. During this level I made notes of decisions and my thought process. This first level of phase 3 was complete when I felt that all the coded data was adequately represented by the thematic map.

At the next level of this phase, I determined how well the individual themes fit within the overall data set and I re-read the entire data set to re-examine the themes and re-coded any new themes that emerged. Finally, I reviewed the thematic map for completeness and accuracy. By the end of this phase, the researcher has identified the major themes and understood how they correlated with one another. (Braun & Clarke, 2023; Kiger & Varpio, 2020).

Figure 3

Example of Thematic Map Used in Phase 4

Visual Thematic Map based for Stage 4 of Thematic Analysis

```
┌──────────────────────────┐
│ Change Management &      │
│ Implementation (n=6)     │
└──────────────────────────┘
        │
Staff Training | Phased Rollout | Early Involvement & Communication

┌──────────────────────────┐
│ External Support &       │
│ Vendor Assistance (6)    │
└──────────────────────────┘
        │
Vendor Support | Onboarding/Data Migration | Software Updates

┌──────────────────────────┐
│ Staff Perceptions of     │
│     Technology (5)       │
└──────────────────────────┘
        │
PU (Usefulness) | PEOU (Ease of Use) | Anxiety/Confidence

┌──────────────────────────┐
│ Leadership & Communication (4) │
└──────────────────────────┘
        │
Transparency | Shared Vision | Feedback Loops

┌──────────────────────────┐
│ Student/Outcome Impact (3) │
└──────────────────────────┘
        │
Engagement | Equity Concerns | Motivation
```

Phase 5: Defining and Renaming Themes

This phase occurred once I was satisfied with the accuracy and coherence of the thematic map. The researcher then refines and clarifies each theme, establishing its meaning and specifying the portion of the data it reflects (Braun & Clarke, 2006; Braun & Clarke, 2023). During this phase of data analysis, I developed comprehensive descriptions of each theme and determined whether subthemes were present. Upon completion, I clearly defined the meaning, scope, and content of each theme within the context of the project. The researcher assigns names to each theme, providing readers with a clear indication of what each theme represented (Kiger & Varpio, 2020).

Phase 6: Producing the Report

This is the phase in which I wrote the project report. At this stage, I had developed a well-defined set of themes. The report was prepared using thematic analysis to enable readers to discern the validity of the analysis. The final report was concise, coherent, logical, and non-repetitive, clearly articulated the narrative conveyed by the data both within and across themes. The report also includes sufficient evidence of the themes within the data, supported by illustrative examples (Braun & Clarke, 2006; Braun & Clarke, 2023).

During the reporting phase, which occurred after the completion of the proposal, I aligned the themes that emerged from the data analysis with both established and recent literature. These themes were integrated within the conceptual framework to strengthen the interpretation of findings. I then proceeded to perform the following tasks:

Update the Literature Review

The researcher conducted a thorough review of recent publications to ensure that the analysis incorporated the latest research. Using academic databases such as PubMed, JSTOR, Google Scholar, and other databases within the Walden University library, I searched for studies published after the proposal had been written and updated the literature review accordingly.

Comparative Analysis

The researcher created a matrix to map the identified themes against the findings from the literature. Next, I reviewed recent studies and examined them in the context of the research question. This comparison helped to identify areas of alignment and divergence between the current data and existing studies (s

Table 3

Matrix Map Identifying Themes Against Findings from the Literature

Identified theme	Findings from the literature	Key supporting sources
Change management and implementation	Phased rollouts, staff training, early involvement, and communication improve adoption	Venkatesh and Bala (2008), Chatzoglou et al. (2015), Gilliam (2022)
External support and vendor assistance	Vendor onboarding, troubleshooting, and updates reduce failures	Mediaty et al. (2025), Meiryani (2014), Ongwae et al. (2021)
Staff perception of technology	PU and PEOU drive adoption; training reduces anxiety and increases acceptance	Davis (1989), Venkatesh and Davis (2000), Tahar et al. (2020)
Leadership and communication	Strong leadership, transparency, and feedback improve organizational readiness	Kotter (2012), Alsharari (2022), Venkatesh and Bala (2008)
Student/Outcome impact	Technology increases engagement but inequities affect outcomes	Baig et al. (2020), Al-Okaily (2024), Priyono and Moin (2023)
Security, privacy, and fraud prevention	AIS improves data protection and reduces fraud risk	Centobelli et al. (2022), Nguyen and Nguyen (2022), Alawida et al. (2022)

Cost and financial barriers	Costs of subscriptions, training, and maintenance limit adaptation	Wahyuni (2023), Holler (2025), Vysochan et al. (2021)
System integration and compatibility issues	Integration with legacy systems is difficult and costly	Marnewick and Labuschagne (2020), Gartner (2023)
Strategic planning and business growth	AIS improves budgeting, forecasting, and long-term growth	AlQershi (2021), Sharma et al. (2023)
COVID-19 and digital transformation	Pandemic accelerated digital adoption; tech-ready businesses survived more easily	Al-Okaily (2024), Baig et al. (2020), Holl and Rama (2024)

Incorporate New Studies

I included insights from new studies to provide a comprehensive understanding of the research topic. The conceptual framework of the TAM served as the foundation for the project, guiding the research questions and analysis. Integrating the identified themes with TAM involved creating a conceptual map and synthesizing the data within the theoretical constructs through conceptual mapping and narrative synthesis. The researcher links the key themes to the components of TAM and writes a detailed narrative explaining how the themes aligned with the model, incorporating examples from the data, and referencing both new and existing literature on TAM (Braun et al., 2022).

The integration of key themes with the existing literature and conceptual framework represented a deliberate and rigorous process that strengthened the data analysis in this qualitative project. Through the systematic exploration of major themes, revision of the literature review, and alignment of findings with the conceptual framework, I produced a project that was methodologically sound, comprehensive, and contextually relevant. This integrative approach bolsters the credibility and dependability of the results while positioning the project within the larger body of scholarly research
(Braun et al., 2022).

In compliance with Walden University's policy, all participants' data were securely maintained and will be stored in a locked safe for a minimum of five years, accessible only to the researcher. Upon the completion of this retention period, the data will be permanently destroyed through shredding to ensure confidentiality and ethical data management. (Walden IRB Manual, 2024).

Reliability and Validity

Reliability

It was imperative that the reliability and validity of the data collection process and instruments are enhanced. This was accomplished through the use of multiple data collection techniques. The interview process was guided by the interview protocol to ensure reliability, which served as the first data collection technique used in the project. In addition, recording the interviews further enhanced the reliability and validity of the data, as the recordings allowed the researcher to capture participants' responses verbatim and enabled the researcher to focus on asking probing questions to elicit rich, detailed data for the project (Knott et al., 2022).

Another way I enhanced the validity and reliability of the data collection instruments was by completing a one-page interview memorandum comprising three sections. This was done immediately after each interview. In the first section, I captured the ethnographic details of the interview by identifying two or three significant moments and describing what occurred during those moments, including participants' facial expressions, gestures, and tone of voice. The second section of the interview memo, which served as the analytical section, contained notes on how the participant's responses diverged from those of other participants, except in the case of the first interview. The third section of the memo functioned as the methodological section, in which the researcher recorded personal reflections on the researcher-participant relationship. (Knott et al., 2020; Yadav, 2022).

Reliability

In research, reliability refers to the stability of the data collection instrument and whether the research instruments measure the same thing in the same way in repeated tests (Connaway et al., 2022). The manner in which the researcher chooses to address the reliability of the qualitative research data is paramount to the dependability of the data.

Dependability

Dependability was a crucial aspect of the project that ensured the consistency and repeatability of the findings. I addressed dependability by employing strategies that verified the stability and consistency of both the data and the overall research process. As the researcher, I used various methods to address dependability in the project. The dependability strategies included member checking, transcript review, maintaining an audit trail, and utilizing triangulation.

Transcript Review

Transcript review constituted a respondent validation technique through which the researcher presented data interpretations and findings to the participants (Rowlands, 2021). This process served to confirm the accuracy and credibility of the researcher's transcription of the participant data. According to Rowlands (2021), transcript review is a critical step in qualitative research, as it enhances the credibility and dependability of the findings. By incorporating participant feedback, the researcher corrects any misinterpretations and confirmed that the results accurately reflected the participants' perspectives. (Lloyd et al., 2024). After transcript review I did not modify my themes because this not no necessary.

Transcript review was conducted to ensure the accuracy, credibility, and trustworthiness of the study's findings. After initial data analysis, each participant received a summary of their interview responses. Participants were invited to review the information, verify that it accurately reflected their perspectives, and provide clarifications or additional insights if needed. Feedback from participants was incorporated into the final analysis, ensuring that the themes and interpretations authentically represented their experiences.

Audit Trail

Maintaining an audit trail is integral to ensuring transparency and rigor in the research process. I documented each stage of data collection, analysis, and decisionmaking in detail, enabling external reviewers to trace and evaluate the methodological path. As Carcary (2020) noted, an audit trail offers a comprehensive record of the researcher's actions and decisions, thereby supporting the assessment of the project's consistency and reproducibility. This systematic documentation functioned as a methodological roadmap for understanding and potentially replicating the research process.

Triangulation

Triangulation involves the use of multiple methods, data sources, or theories to cross-check and validate the findings (Lemon et al., 2020). This approach helped confirm the reliability of both the data and the interpretations. Lemon et al. (2020) argued that triangulation strengthened a project by integrating multiple perspectives, thereby enhancing the credibility and dependability of the findings. By corroborating evidence from different sources such as interviews and public documents, I ensured that the conclusions were well-supported and reliable.

Validity

Validity describes whether the data collection instruments measure what they were intended to measure. In qualitative research, validity refers to the accuracy and trustworthiness of the findings (Connaway et al., 2022). It encompassed the extent to which the research measures what it purported to measure and how well the findings represent the reality of the participants' experiences and perspectives (Connaway et al., 2022). To ensure the rigor and trustworthiness of this qualitative project, I focused on credibility, transferability, confirmability, and data saturation.

Credibility

Credibility refers to the confidence in the truth of the data and the interpretations (Karkar et al., 2023) It involves ensuring that the research findings accurately represent the participants' experiences and viewpoints. Techniques such as triangulation, member checking, and prolonged engagement are used to enhance credibility (Kakar et al., 2023). One way researchers promote credibility is through the use of various triangulation processes, which involve utilizing multiple sources of information or procedures from the data to repeatedly establish identifiable patterns (Stahl & King, 2020).

Credibility in this study was established through multiple strategies that ensured the accuracy and trustworthiness of the findings. The researcher used prolonged engagement with the data, carefully reviewing transcripts and conducting iterative rounds of coding to develop a deep understanding of participant experiences. Member checking was implemented by sharing summarized interpretations with participants to verify accuracy and confirm that the themes reflected their intended meanings. Triangulation of data sources, such as comparing interview responses, researcher notes, and literature, further strengthened the consistency of the findings. Additionally, maintaining an audit trail of decisions made throughout the research process enhanced transparency and supported the credibility of the study's conclusions.

Transferability

Transferability refers to the extent to which the findings of the project could be applied to other contexts. Several strategies were employed to ensure transferability in this project, including providing detailed and rich descriptions of the research context, participants, and topic; selecting participants and settings relevant to the research purpose; and clearly outlining the context in which the project was conducted. Transferability involved describing the cultural, social, and environmental factors that may have influenced the findings of the project (Stalmeijer, 2024).

Confirmability

Confirmability pertains to the degree to which the findings are shaped by the participants rather than by researcher bias, motivation, or personal interest (Dahal, 2023). Techniques such as maintaining a reflexive journal, conducting peer debriefing, and establishing an audit trail help ensure confirmability by demonstrating that the findings were grounded in the data (Dahal, 2023).

Confirmability was achieved by ensuring that the study's findings were grounded in the participants' perspectives rather than the researcher's assumptions or biases. To support this, the researcher maintained a detailed audit trail that documented methodological decisions, coding processes, and theme development throughout the study. Reflexive journaling was used to identify and bracket personal assumptions that could influence data interpretation. Member checking further supported confirmability by allowing participants to verify the accuracy of the interpretations. Together, these strategies demonstrated that the findings were data-driven, transparent, and could be independently traced and reviewed by other researchers.

Data Saturation

Data saturation refers to the point in data collection at which no new information or themes emerge from the data (Mwita, 2022). Ensuring data saturation was crucial for maintaining the comprehensiveness and completeness of the project. Strategies I used to achieve data saturation included the following. First, I continuously collected and analyzed the data until no new themes or information emerged. This iterative process helped in identifying when data saturation was reached (Fusch & Ness, 2015). Second, I ensured an adequate and diverse sample size that captured the complexity of the phenomenon under project for this qualitative project. Sample size and diversity enhanced the likelihood of reaching data saturation (Braun & Clarke, 2021). I also regularly reviewed and reflected on the data to assess whether new information was still emerging. Regular review and reflection helped in determining the point of data saturation (Guest et al., 2020).

These strategies collectively strengthened the achievement of data saturation by ensuring that the themes developed were both comprehensive and firmly grounded in participants' experiences. The iterative process of simultaneous data collection and analysis allowed the researcher to monitor emerging patterns continuously and recognize when additional interviews were no longer producing new insights. Incorporating a diverse sample further contributed to saturation by capturing a wide range of perspectives and reducing the likelihood that important viewpoints were overlooked. Regular review and reflection ensured ongoing assessment of the data's depth and completeness, helping to confirm that the dataset was sufficiently rich to support credible and well-substantiated findings. Together, these practices demonstrated methodological rigor and reinforced the trustworthiness of the study's conclusions.

Transition and Summary

In Section 3, I described the role of the researcher, defined the population and identified participants. The sampling method that I used to select the participants and the reasons using such a sampling method were also discussed. The research methodology and design have been carefully described in detail, and an in-depth look at the *Belmont Report* and the ethical principles governing the project were also discussed. How I would handle biases were also addressed and the informed consent form was discussed as well as where to find it in the project. In this section I described in detail the data collection instruments and techniques and justified my reasons for the selections. In addition, I outlined how the research instruments and techniques would be used to enhance the reliability and validity of the project. I also outlined the data analysis and data organization techniques in detail. Finally, in this section, I outlined the validity and reliability of the project as well as how to ensure that data saturation was achieved.

Section 4: Findings and Conclusions

This project was guided by the research question: What strategies do small business owners use to effectively implement new accounting software to remain competitive and profitable? This section begins with a detailed presentation of the research findings, providing insight into participant responses, thematic analysis, and alignment with the project's central research question. Each participant in this project operates or is the manager of a small business in Tennessee. Some of the participants' responses to the interview questions were in keeping with the conceptual framework and literature. I reviewed the participants' company websites and the interview transcripts for the purpose of conducting triangulation and to ensure reliability of the research data.

While conducting the interviews, the participants willingly shared their views, ideas, and experiences, and I took notes and recorded the interview responses. I verified my interpretation of participants responses in follow-up visits and employed member checking to confirm the validity of the responses. Member checking improves the accuracy, validity and credibility of qualitative research results (Lloyd et al., 2024). I reviewed research data while focusing on the use of strategies and the reliance on new or updated accounting software used in small businesses and how the owners utilize the software to be profitable, leading to competitive advantage for the businesses. The TAM was the conceptual framework for this project because it explains how employees accept and use new or updated technology that has been implemented in organizations (Davis, 1989).

Presentation of the Findings

In this section of the project, I present the findings of the research. I discuss how the participants responded to the selected themes, how the data addressed the research question, and align the findings with the existing research. Utilizing Braun and Clark's 6step approach, with NVivo version 14 software verification, I analyzed the data and identified themes from the data. The five main themes emerged from the data analysis: (a) change management and organizational culture, (b) the importance of external support and strategic partnerships, (c) measuring effectiveness through operational and client metrics, (d) challenges and overcoming barriers, and (e) business sustainability, agility and lessons learned (see Table 4).

Table 4

Frequency of Themes Identified Across Participants

Variable (Theme)	P1	P2	P3	P4	P5	P6	Total Frequency
Change management and organizational culture	4	3	2	2	3	3	17
Importance of external support and strategic partnerships	3	3	2	2	3	3	16
Measuring effectiveness through operational and client metrics	3	3	3	2	3	3	17
Challenges and overcoming barriers	4	4	3	3	3	3	20
Business sustainability and lessons learned	3	3	3	2	2	3	16

Note. The table presents the frequency with which each participant referenced the identified themes during the interview process. Totals indicate the overall number of references across all participants ($N = 6$).

Theme 1: Change Management and Organizational Culture

All six participants emphasized that successful implementation of their accounting software required much more than just installing a system. For example, P1 stated, "I purchased an accounting software to keep track of our financial records so that the business and the recording procedures can go smoothly." The participants also noted that successful implementation of their accounting software demands a cultural and organizational shift within each of their small businesses. P3 added, "we addressed challenges through comprehensive training programs and by designating 'super users' within the team who provided peer support." Similarly, Participant 4 noted, "incremental training helped staff build confidence gradually."

Both P1 and P2 highlighted the importance of involving their staff early in the implementation process while also fostering a work atmosphere of open communication which aligns with the TAM concept of PEOU, which made employees more likely to accept an accounting system which they accept and so will show their support in learning such a system (Davis,

1989). P1 stated “involving our staff early in the process and keeping communication open made a tremendous difference. Once everyone understood the purpose behind the change, resistance faded and collaboration grew stronger.” P3 discussed designating *super users* to mentor peers during implementation, thereby reducing the learning curve, “we addressed challenges through comprehensive training programs and by designating *super users* within the team who provided peer support.” While P4 emphasized incremental training sessions to gradually build staff confidence by stating, “incremental training helped staff build confidence gradually.” P6 noted the importance of balancing efficient improvements with personalized client services, which is closely aligned with the TAM PU principle that directly influences employees’ behavioral intention to use technology, “while software improves efficiency, our success lies in maintaining trust and personal relationships that have been the foundation of our family business for over four decades.” Gupta (2025) similarly noted that business owners or managers must visualize the end result of the software implementation in mind so they can cultivate an organizational culture amongst employees which will embrace change and the mindset to adopt new workflows.

These practices reduced resistance to change and cultivated a culture of learning, reinforcing the TAM idea that usability perceptions directly influence behavioral intention to use technology. P6 highlighted the importance of balancing efficiency with client service by stating, "while software improves efficiency, our success lies in maintaining trust and personal relationships that have been the foundation of our family business for over four decades."

Correlation to the Literature. The findings of the project align closely with existing literature on AIS and the adoption of technology by small businesses. Consistent with Diavastis et al. (2024), the participants emphasized that successful implementation of accounting software requires strategic planning, structured training, and the involvement of all the major stakeholders. The project results were also corroborated by Jensen (2018), who likened software adoption to a home renovation, highlighting that it requires a clear vision, phased execution, and continuous improvement. Nguyen et al. (2024) noted that the participants identified cost, training, and integration challenges as significant barriers, demonstrating that financial and human resource constraints continue to hinder full technological adoption in small businesses. The findings further support the conclusions of Kraus et al. (2022), who noted that change management is a critical success factor, as roughly 70% of technological change initiatives fail due to resistance. In this project, early staff involvement, open communication, and ongoing vendor support reduced that resistance and promoted user confidence. Overall, the results are consistent with previous research showing that effective AIS implementation in small firms enhances accuracy, efficiency, and client satisfaction (Kraus et al., 2022).

Beyond confirming existing findings, this project expands on prior research by providing updated, qualitative insight into how small business owners apply change management and continuous learning in real-world accounting software implementation. While previous studies often focused on large organizations or quantitative performance measures, this research highlights the lived experiences of small business owners navigating limited budgets, staff resistance, and evolving technology. The emphasis the participants placed on vendor collaboration, phased rollouts, and ongoing staff development adds new depth to the literature by showing that sustained success depends on adaptability and cultural readiness, not merely system selection. Furthermore, this project underscores the human aspect of AIS adoption, bridging a gap in the literature by demonstrating that emotional readiness and confidence are as vital as technical preparedness in achieving effective implementation outcomes.

Correlation to the Conceptual Framework. The TAM by Davis (1989) served as the guiding framework for this project. The findings strongly correlate with the TAM's core constructs of perceived usefulness and perceived ease of use. Participants confirmed that employees' willingness to adopt accounting software depended largely on their belief that the system would make their work more efficient and reliable, reflecting perceived usefulness. Similarly, hands-on training, vendor support, and user-friendly software features enhanced perceived ease of use, thereby increasing overall acceptance. The data also support Venkatesh et al. (2022), who extended TAM to emphasize the importance of external variables such as social influence and facilitating conditions. This was evident in participants' reports that organizational culture, leadership communication, and vendor collaboration significantly affected adoption success. The alignment between the project's findings and the TAM framework underscores that small business technology adoption is not simply a technical choice, but a behavioral process shaped by users' perceptions, experiences, and environmental support.

This project also extends TAM by illustrating how organizational culture, leadership behavior, and vendor relationships act as external variables that influence perceived usefulness and ease of use. While the TAM traditionally emphasizes individual user perceptions, the findings suggest that collective engagement, through communication, trust-building, and shared accountability, enhances adoption success in small business contexts (Diavastis et al., 2024). By integrating leadership support, team learning, and external facilitation into the TAM framework, this project contributes a more holistic understanding of technology acceptance in small enterprises. These extensions to the TAM reveal that successful AIS adoption is not only driven by cognitive evaluations of usefulness and usability but also by social and contextual factors that shape users' motivation to embrace change. This expanded interpretation strengthens the TAM's applicability to real-world small business environments and provides a foundation for future research to further refine the model within entrepreneurial and SME

contexts.

Theme 2: Importance of External Support and Strategic Partnerships

The participants in this project consistently cited external support from software vendors such as QuickBooks as critical for the successful adoption of this accounting software. P5 shared that "External support was essential. The vendor provided troubleshooting, assisted with integrations, and ensured compliance with insurance billing codes." P2 also emphasized vendor involvement, "We relied on vendor technical support and training to ensure the software worked with our diverse services." P1, P2, and P3 relied heavily on vendor assistance for technical troubleshooting, software updates, and compliance guidance. Participant 5 also shared that, "external support was essential, the vendor provided troubleshooting, assisted with integrations, and ensured compliance with insurance billing codes." These examples align with TAM's PEOU construct, as vendor assistance reduced uncertainty and simplified interaction with the system (Davis, 1989).

Correlation to the Literature. The participants' emphasis on vendor collaboration closely aligns with previous studies that identify external technical support as a vital determinant of successful AIS implementation. Ibrahim et al. (2020) found that coordination among vendors, management, and end users enhances the efficiency of software adoption by ensuring continuous communication and timely problem-solving.

Similarly, Religia et al. (2021) argued that small firms that cultivate long-term partnerships with software providers gain superior knowledge transfer and postimplementation assistance, which, in turn, increases system reliability and user confidence. The experiences of Participants 1 through 5 confirm these findings, as vendor support in troubleshooting, compliance, and integration reduced uncertainty and strengthened PEOU which is one of the central constructs of TAM (Davis, 1989). Huerta and Jensen (2017) further noted that effective external collaboration bridges the gap between technical potential and practical application, a point mirrored in this project as vendors helped small businesses tailor systems to their specific service models. Collectively, these parallels reinforce that strategic vendor partnerships are not ancillary but foundational to sustain AIS success in small business environments.

Correlation to the Conceptual Framework. Under TAM, PEOU is enhanced when external support simplifies system interaction and reduces uncertainty (Davis & Venkatesh, 1996). P4 reinforced the importance of internal support, stating, “We assigned an internal 'software champion' who served as the point of contact for questions and troubleshooting." Together, these strategies show how small businesses leverage external and internal resources to enhance adoption success, reflecting the literature on strategic coordination in AIS implementation. Ibrahim et al. (2020) noted that the strategic coordination of technology, organizational processes, and stakeholders is the key to the successful implementation of any AIS system. All of the participants relied on the vendor's expertise which demonstrates how external support can directly influence both the adoption acceptance and smooth functioning of accounting software in the real world of small businesses.

Theme 3: Measuring Effectiveness Through Operational Client Metrics

The participants in this project measure the success of their implementation by combining operational indicators such as efficiency, error reduction, and data accuracy, with client-focused metrics such as satisfaction, retention, and clients' responsiveness. P1 reported improvements in payroll and bookkeeping efficiency. P1 noted that "we measured effectiveness by improvements in payroll processing, bookkeeping accuracy, and faster turnaround times for tax filings," while P3 emphasized client satisfaction and regulatory responsiveness. Participant 3 stated, "key metrics included client retention rates, steady revenue growth, and positive client feedback." P5 used real-time financial reporting to identify trends while proactively adjusting operations and highlighted the role of real-time financial reporting, noting that, "the software's built-in compliance update prevented a large number of potential claim rejections." P3 also stated, "key metrics included client retention rates, steady revenue growth, and positive client feedback."

From a TAM perspective, PU is validated when the system produces tangible improvements in daily operations and supports organizational tools, when users see concrete improvements in efficiency and outcomes (Davis, 1989). Sarsiti (2019) noted that strategic AIS implementation must include monitoring metrics to ensure the technology meets business needs, thereby reinforcing the link between system effectiveness and employee acceptance which will justify continued investment in technology.

Correlation to the Literature. The findings in this project are strongly supported by existing research emphasizing the importance of using both operational and clientcentered indicators to measure the effectiveness of AIS. Sarsiti (2019) maintained that monitoring measurable performance outcomes, such as processing efficiency, accuracy, and client responsiveness, is essential to justify technological investments and sustain user commitment. Wahyudi and Antonio (2024) similarly argued that continuous measurement of financial and customer-driven results ensures that technology remains aligned with business goals and market demands.

Participants in this project demonstrated that combining quantitative measures for example, error reduction, faster payroll, revenue growth with qualitative assessments such as client satisfaction, trust, and retention yields a comprehensive picture of success (Ibrahim et al., 2020). The participants' experiences also echo Ibrahim et al. (2020), who found that integrating feedback mechanisms and performance dashboards promotes transparency and continuous improvement. Collectively, this body of evidence affirms that rigorous, data-driven evaluation strengthens accountability, enhances organizational learning, and reinforces employee confidence in the accounting system's value.

Correlation to the Conceptual Framework. TAM provides a clear lens through which to interpret these findings. According to Davis (1989), PU is validated when technology demonstrably enhances job performance or organizational outcomes. Each participant described tangible benefits—improved efficiency, reduced claim rejections, and greater client satisfaction—that directly reflect this construct. When users experience measurable gains in accuracy and speed, their confidence in and willingness to continue using the system increase, fulfilling the model's behavioral-intention pathway.

The findings also align with the extended TAM perspective, which posited that outcome quality and feedback loops reinforce both PU and Perceived Ease of Use over time

(Venkatesh et al., 2022). By employing metrics to verify system effectiveness, organizational leaders strengthen the feedback cycle that sustains user engagement and long-term acceptance. Thus, this project contributes to the conceptual framework by demonstrating that continuous performance measurement not only validates technological usefulness but also institutionalizes trust in AIS as an indispensable strategic tool for small business growth and resilience.

Theme 4: Challenges and Overcoming Barriers

All six participants faced similar barriers, including staff resistance, data migration issues, technical integration challenges, and workflow adaptation. P2 mitigated these issues through the use of rolled-out phases and hands-on training. Participant 2 shared, "Some staff initially struggled with adapting to new workflows, and the breadth of features required a learning curve." Participant 6 added, "we conducted thorough training sessions and offered continuous support to staff to ease the transition." P4 emphasized continuous communication and internal support to address employees' concerns, Participant 4 stated, "ongoing communication, incremental training, and internal 'software champion' support helped overcome challenges." These approaches mirror the literature on overcoming barriers through change management, pilot testing, and staff involvement (SBA, 2020).

Correlation to the Literature. The findings from this project are consistent with prior research emphasizing that small businesses frequently face barriers such as resistance to change, technical integration challenges, and insufficient training when implementing new accounting systems. Ivanov and Petrova (2024) highlighted that employee reluctance often stems from fear of technological complexity or job displacement, underscoring the importance of gradual rollouts and clear communication. Similarly, the Small Business Administration (SBA, 2020) found that phased implementation, pilot testing, and consistent staff engagement are effective strategies to mitigate resistance and foster acceptance. The participants' use of hands-on training, internal champions, and continuous communication aligns with these recommendations and supports the view that success in AIS adoption depends as much on human factors as on technical readiness. Huerte and Jensen (2017) also noted that businesses that invest in structured change management and iterative testing experience smoother transitions and higher long-term adoption rates. Collectively, the literature supports the conclusion that overcoming implementation barriers requires integrating technical support, employee empowerment, and leadership commitment to sustain innovation.

Correlation to the Conceptual Framework. According to TAM, addressing PEOU is critical in overcoming resistance and employees are more likely to adopt technology if obstacles are minimized and support is accessible (Davis, 1989). The extant literature highlights that small businesses encounter cost concerns, integration problems, and resistance to change which align with the participants' experiences (Ivanov & Petrova, 2024; SBA, 2024). In addition, effective change management and modular training, help mitigate these barriers and increase acceptance.

TAM provides a valuable lens for understanding how the participants' experiences with overcoming barriers influence technology adoption. According to Davis (1989), PEOU plays a pivotal role in reducing user resistance, when employees feel that a system is easy to learn and support is accessible, their likelihood of adoption increases. The participants' reliance on structured training, open communication, and the creation of *software champions* directly addressed PEOU by simplifying the learning process and minimizing anxiety associated with change. These findings also resonate with extended TAM research (Venkatesh et al., 2022), which introduced facilitating conditions and organizational support as external factors that enhance user confidence. By implementing incremental training and fostering a supportive learning environment, participants effectively bridged the gap between technical potential and user acceptance (Venkatesh et al., 2022). This alignment reinforces TAM's premise that successful adoption requires more than system design, it depends on how organizational leaders manage human attitudes and experiences throughout the implementation process.

Theme 5: Business Sustainability, Agility and Lesson Learned

Software adoption not only enhanced efficiency but also contributed to business resilience and competitiveness. Participant 3 noted, "advanced reporting allowed us to quickly identify and address discrepancies in cash flow, enabling proactive client advisories that prevented costly penalties." Participant 5 similarly stated, "we monitored revenue stability, reduced claim rejections, and consistent patient payment turnaround times during and after the software transition." These statements illustrated how software adoption extended beyond routine efficiency gains to directly support organizational stability and competitive positioning. Participants described improved visibility into financial performance, which enabled faster detection of issues and more informed decision-making. The ability to proactively address cash-flow discrepancies and reduce claim rejections demonstrated that technology strengthened operational control, reduced risk, and enhanced service reliability. Collectively, these outcomes signaled that accounting software adoption functioned as both a strategic and protective mechanism for small businesses.

Participant 6 reinforced the people-first approach, "the importance of blending technology with personalized client service cannot be overstated." TAM's behavioral intention to use is influenced by PU, and participants confirmed that technology adoption supported strategic decision-making, risk mitigation, and sustainable growth. Participant 1 emphasized lessons learned, "accounting systems are vital to organizations…they convert raw data into information for management decision-making." These insights align with the literature suggesting that continuous monitoring, feedback, and staff involvement increase acceptance and long-term effectiveness (Ibrahim et al., 2020;
Huerte & Jensen, 2017).

Correlation to the Literature. The findings from this project are consistent with the literature emphasizing that technology adoption strengthens business sustainability and competitiveness when supported by continuous learning and adaptability. Jensen (2018) asserted that accounting software implementation enhances long-term resilience by allowing firms to respond swiftly to financial discrepancies, market fluctuations, and regulatory changes. Ibrahim et al. (2020) similarly noted that small businesses leveraging technology-driven data analytics gain strategic advantages by transforming raw financial data into actionable insights for decision-making. Participants in this project demonstrated these principles through their use of advanced reporting to detect cash flow issues and improve revenue stability. Moreover, the literature supports the participants' people-centered approach, and TAM offers a useful lens for interpreting these findings through the constructs of (PU) and Behavioral Intention to Use (BI). According to Davis (1989), users' intention to use technology is driven by their belief that it enhances performance and supports organizational objectives. In this project, participants reported that software adoption improved decision-making, reduced financial risk, and strengthened long-term sustainability which are key indicators of

PU. As participants experienced tangible operational benefits, their behavioral intention to continue using and investing in technology grew stronger. This relationship mirrors the extended TAM proposed by Venkatesh et al. (2022), which integrates external factors such as trust, user satisfaction, and organizational support.

The participants' emphasis on balancing technological efficiency with personalized client service further expands TAM's relevance, demonstrating that sustained adoption depends not only on perceived functionality but also on how technology complements human-centered business values. This synthesis reinforces TAM as a robust explanatory framework for understanding the link between technological innovation, user acceptance, and small business resilience. Wahyudi and Antonio (2024) found that aligning technology with human relationships and clientfocused strategies promotes trust, retention, and business longevity. Collectively, the participants' practices and the scholarly evidence converge on the idea that technology is not merely an operational tool but a strategic asset for sustaining growth, improving service quality, and fostering innovation.

Correlation to the Conceptual Framework. TAM offers a useful lens for interpreting these findings through the constructs of PU and BI. According to Davis (1989), users' intention to use technology is driven by their belief that it enhances performance and supports organizational objectives. In this project, participants reported that software adoption improved decision-making, reduced financial risk, and strengthened long-term sustainability, key indicators of PU. As participants experienced tangible operational benefits, their behavioral intention to continue using and investing in technology grew stronger. This relationship mirrors the extended TAM proposed by Venkatesh et al. (2022), which integrates external factors such as trust, user satisfaction, and organizational support. The participants' emphasis on balancing technological efficiency with personalized client service further expands TAM's relevance, demonstrating that sustained adoption depends not only on perceived functionality but also on how technology complements human-centered business values. This synthesis reinforces TAM as a robust explanatory framework for understanding the link between technological innovation, user acceptance, and small business resilience.

Business Contributions and Recommendations for Professional Practice

This project contributes significantly to the professional practice of business by demonstrating how small business leaders can successfully adopt AIS to enhance operational efficiency, sustain competitiveness, and strengthen long-term resilience. The findings confirmed that technology adoption is not solely a technical decision, but a strategic and behavioral process influenced by organizational culture, leadership, and staff engagement. Grounded in the TAM, the project validated that *PU and PEOU* are central to technology acceptance and continued utilization. Participants highlighted that vendor partnerships, effective change management, and structured training are vital to reducing implementation challenges and improving user confidence. These insights expand professional practice by linking theoretical acceptance constructs to actionable strategies that small business leaders can employ to improve technology integration and business outcomes.

Filling Gaps in Professional Practice

Prior studies have often examined AIS adoption in large organizations, leaving a knowledge gap regarding small business practices (Ivanov & Petrova, 2024). This project addressed that gap by offering a nuanced understanding of how small business owners navigate software implementation with limited financial and human resources. The findings show that even within smaller operational structures, success can be achieved when leaders align implementation strategies with human-centered approaches, early staff involvement, continuous training, and communication transparency. The evidence reinforces that perceived value drives behavioral intention, echoing the TAM framework, and demonstrates how technology can enhance productivity, client satisfaction, and financial stability (Venkatesh et al., 2022). These insights extend the body of knowledge by showing that user acceptance in small firms depends not only on technical usability but also on leadership engagement and ongoing support systems.

Practical Recommendations for Business Leaders

Adopt Structured Change Management Practices

Small business leaders should implement phased rollouts that include pilot testing, feedback loops, and visible leadership support to minimize resistance. Incremental implementation allows employees to develop competence and confidence over time, enhancing PEOU and sustained adoption.

Invest in Comprehensive and Ongoing Training

Training should not end after the initial launch. Regular refresher sessions and peer mentoring programs can ensure employees remain competent as software updates evolve. Training increases both PU and PEOU, which are critical for maintaining user trust and engagement.

Leverage Vendor Partnerships and External Support

Collaborating with software vendors, consultants, or IT specialists ensures that business leaders maximize the system's potential while minimizing downtime. Vendor support enhances implementation quality, technical customization, and compliance accuracy.

Integrate Performance Metrics into Technology Evaluation

Leaders should track operational and client-centered indicators such as processing speed, accuracy, customer satisfaction, and retention to evaluate technology effectiveness. These metrices create accountability and data driven decision-making aligned with the TAM construct of usefulness.

Balance Technology with Human-Centered Practices

The participants' success illustrates that technology adoption should complement, not replace human relationships. Personalized service, staff empowerment, and transparent communication foster trust and strengthen organizational culture, factors essential for long-term business resilience.

Knowledge Dissemination

The results of this research can be disseminated through professional conferences, small business workshops, and academic forums focused on entrepreneurship, accounting, and technology integration. Training programs sponsored by small business associations and community colleges could also incorporate these findings into professional development curricula for entrepreneurs.

Furthermore, peer-reviewed journals such as *The Journal of Small Business Management* or *International Journal of Accounting Information Systems* would provide an ideal platform to expand scholarly discussion on TAM and small business technology adoption. Ultimately, this bridges the gap between theory and practice by transforming academic constructs into actionable business strategies. It empowers small business leaders to make informed, evidence-based decisions when adopting accounting systems that enhance efficiency, strengthen competitiveness, and promote organizational sustainability.

Implications

The findings of this project make several significant contributions to the professional practice of business, particularly in the adoption and effective use of AIS in SMEs. The results reinforce TAM, which emphasizes that PEOU and

PU are central drivers of technology adoption (Davis, 1989; Venkatesh et al., 2022). Across all six participants, the consistent application of training, external support, and incremental implementation illustrated how businesses can minimize resistance, build confidence, and translate technology into sustainable operational improvements.

A first key contribution lies in the confirmation that change management practices directly shape technology success. Participants highlighted training, peer mentoring, and phased rollouts as essential for overcoming resistance. These findings support recent literature suggesting that small businesses often fail not because of inadequate technology but because of poor implementation strategies (Kraus et al., 2022). By framing AIS adoption as both a technical and cultural shift, this research fills a gap in the literature by providing practitioner-based evidence that technology acceptance is inseparable from organizational learning.

Second, this project contributes to practice by showing how vendor partnerships and external support structures are vital in sustaining adoption. For SMEs with limited inhouse expertise, reliance on vendors, consultants, and internal software *champions* was a recurring theme. This insight underscores the need for business leaders to cultivate strong partnerships with technology providers. Recent research by Awa et al. (2015), highlighted that collaborative vendor-client relationships improve long-term system utilization and ROI, which echoes the lived experiences of the participants in this project.

Third, the research contributes practical knowledge on how businesses can measure technological effectiveness through operational and client-centered metrics.

Participants monitored payroll efficiency, billing accuracy, claim rejection rates, and client retention to assess the value of AIS investments. These findings respond to calls in the literature for more actionable frameworks for technology performance evaluation in SMEs (Gunasekaran et al., 2022). By linking AIS adoption to tangible outcomes such as reduced errors, faster processing, and improved client trust, this research provides a roadmap for business leaders to translate abstract system goals into measurable business benefits.

Implications for Social Change

Beyond the professional practice of business, this project carries meaningful implications for social change at the individual, organizational, and community levels. AIS adoption in small businesses not only enhances profitability and efficiency but also promotes broader social well-being through transparency, accountability, and access to opportunity.

At the individual level, participants emphasized how training and peer mentoring empowered employees by reducing anxiety and developing new digital skills. This process builds professional confidence and employability, which supports workforce development and upward mobility. As highlighted by recent studies, digital literacy is a cornerstone of modern economic participation, and equipping employees with AIS skills contributes to inclusive growth (Kraus et al., 2022). These findings demonstrated that AIS adoption functioned not only as a business improvement strategy but also as a catalyst for social empowerment. By equipping employees with digital competencies and reducing technology-related anxiety, small businesses contributed to individual skillbuilding that extended beyond the workplace. This increased capacity enhanced employees' employability and long-term career mobility, reinforcing the role of technology adoption as a driver of equitable workforce development. As participants gained confidence and proficiency, the benefits radiated outward supporting stronger organizational cultures and contributing to more digitally resilient communities.

At the organizational level, AIS adoption fosters greater financial integrity and compliance, which strengthens stakeholder trust. Accurate reporting reduces the risk of fraud, mismanagement, and compliance penalties, thereby protecting both businesses and their clients. By improving reliability and transparency, SMEs can build stronger client relationships and more ethical practices, reinforcing a culture of accountability (Sharma et al., 2022).

At the community and societal level, sustainable SMEs play a vital role in promoting economic resilience and job creation. When businesses leverage AIS to streamline operations and remain competitive, they are better positioned to expand services, hire employees, and invest in community growth (Sharma et al., 2022). Furthermore, improved compliance and financial reporting contribute to tax revenues that support public services, extending the social impact beyond the business itself.

Finally, the findings support the notion of technology as an equalizer. SMEs often face disadvantages compared to large corporations due to limited resources, but accessible accounting technologies narrow this gap. By demonstrating how SMEs can adopt AIS effectively through training, vendor support, and cultural change, this research promotes social equity in business practice. It affirms the worth, dignity, and development of smaller enterprises and the communities they sustain, aligning with broader goals of sustainable economic development (Awa et al., 2015; Venkatesh et al., 2003).

Recommendations for Further Research

Based on these findings, several recommendations for further research can be made for business leaders, managers, and policymakers in the following areas. First, leaders should integrate change management into AIS adoption. Leaders should anticipate employee resistance and proactively design training, peer support, and phased implementation plans. Assigning "software champions" within departments can create localized expertise and reduce adoption anxiety.

It is also recommended to build strong vendor partnerships. SMEs should establish ongoing contracts with vendors that go beyond initial setup to include training, troubleshooting, compliance updates, and integration support. These partnerships not only reduce technical risks but also improve staff confidence in system reliability.

Third, leaders should develop multi-dimensional performance metrics. Business owners should measure AIS effectiveness through a balance of operational efficiency, for example, reduced errors, faster payroll, compliance accuracy particularly, adherence to tax codes and claim acceptance, in addition to positive client in the areas of client retention and client satisfaction. These metrics ensure the software supports both internal processes and external service quality.

Leaders should also encourage cross-industry dissemination and peer learning.

Results should be shared through business conferences, professional associations, and trade journals where SMEs can learn practical implementation strategies. Training modules can be developed in partnership with chambers of commerce or industry groups to broaden awareness.

Finally, leaders should focus on policy level engagement. Policymakers and business development agencies should provide incentives and training grants to encourage SME technology adoption, particularly in underserved industries. These findings highlight that with adequate support, SMEs can leverage AIS to improve competitiveness and sustainability.

Recommendations for Future Research to Improve Practice in Business

These recommendations flow directly from the project's conclusions because effective AIS adoption is not solely about technology selection but about cultivating human, organizational, and strategic conditions for sustained use. Business leaders, SME managers, and vendor partners should all pay attention to these results, while dissemination can occur through academic journals, industry conferences, small business workshops, and government-sponsored training initiatives.

Future researchers could build on this project by using larger and more diverse samples of SMEs across industries to strengthen generalizability, addressing the limitation of the small participant pool noted in Section 1. Expanding the sample size and incorporating medium and large businesses could also provide comparative insights into whether adoption patterns and challenges differ by organizational scale (De Oliveira, 2023). A mixed-methods design that combines interviews with quantitative surveys could provide deeper insights into the relationship between TAM constructs and business performance while reducing participant or researcher bias (Kohler et al., 2022).

In addition, longitudinal studies would help capture how perceptions of usefulness and ease of use change over time, addressing the limitation of cross-sectional data. Future studies might also examine the influence of external factors such as vendor support, government incentives, or industry regulations on AIS adoption, offering both academic and practical contributions. To further address concerns that participants may be reluctant to disclose sensitive information, future researchers might employ strategies such as anonymous surveys or digital data collection methods to encourage more candid responses (Campbell et al., 2022). By addressing these limitations, subsequent studies could provide a more comprehensive and dynamic understanding of technology adoption in small businesses and its impact on long-term business sustainability.

Reflections

This journey has been extraordinarily challenging for me, as I first began this doctoral process in 2014 and had to take several breaks to protect my mental health and navigate significant life events, including the passing of my husband of 23 years. Over time, I developed preconceived ideas and strong attachments to the original structure of the DBA program, and adjusting to the new system has not been easy. For instance, I struggled to accept the expectation of producing a 20-page literature review, as it clashed with the standards of the former DBA model in which I was originally trained. This created a personal bias that I have had to consciously acknowledge and manage as I transitioned into the revised format. I also initially overlooked completing this reflection component because it was not part of my original DBA requirements, and I had to adapt to new expectations that felt unfamiliar.

Additionally, I experienced multiple chair transitions throughout my program, which required ongoing adjustments to new advising styles, communication patterns, and scholarly expectations.

Despite these challenges, I can genuinely say that the process has also been deeply rewarding. I have had to motivate myself through countless difficult moments, giving myself mini-lectures to push forward when the emotional and academic load felt overwhelming. I cried many times, most recently just yesterday, after losing all of the corrections I had completed for my second chair. It was devastating to realize that my autosave had not been enabled, and after falling asleep from exhaustion, my computer shut down, and all of my work vanished. Starting over from scratch was heartbreaking,

yet I did it.

I also encountered challenges with my research participants. Coordinating interviews required patience, flexibility, and respect for their demanding schedules, especially during tax season. I continually sought backup participants in case anyone withdrew, which added another layer of stress. Recruiting and securing participants was one of the most difficult parts of this entire study, and it is not an experience I would voluntarily repeat.

Despite all of this, the process has transformed me, academically, emotionally, and personally. It has tested my resilience and reaffirmed my capacity to persevere in the face of adversity.

Some of the changes I think about now involve embracing flexibility, practicing patience, and allowing myself to grow beyond the expectations I held when I first entered the program in 2014. This journey has reshaped not only my academic identity but also my understanding of perseverance, loss, transformation, and personal strength. While the challenges were significant, the evolution they sparked within me is something I will carry forward into every future endeavor.

Conclusion

In conclusion, this project has provided a comprehensive exploration of the strategies small business owners employ to implement accounting software and sustain competitiveness, with a particular focus on the human and technological factors influencing successful adoption. The findings highlight the critical roles of change management, staff training, external support, and proactive problem-solving in ensuring both operational efficiency and business continuity.

By integrating TAM, the project underscores how perceptions of usefulness and ease of use shape employee acceptance and effective utilization of accounting systems. Despite limitations related to sample size and the scope of business types, the insights gained offer meaningful contributions to professional practice, providing concrete guidance for small business leaders seeking to navigate technology transitions. Ultimately, this research reinforces the value of blending technology with personalized management approaches, demonstrating that sustainable business growth is achieved not solely through software implementation but through the strategic alignment of people, processes, and technology. These findings serve as a foundation for both academic inquiry and practical application, empowering business owners and practitioners to make informed decisions that enhance performance, resilience, and long-term success..

www.ingramcontent.com/pod-product-compliance
Lightning Source LLC
LaVergne TN
LVHW050814061126
851857LV00012B/803
* 9 7 8 5 3 6 3 0 1 7 9 4 0 *